# THE SHOOT LUNCH

The *Tradition*, the *Camaraderie* and the *Craic*

# THE SHOOT LUNCH

The *Tradition*, the *Camaraderie* and the *Craic*

J C Jeremy Hobson

ILLUSTRATIONS BY MANDY SHEPHERD

Quiller

## Publisher's Note

*Craic* – a term for enjoyment, fun, good company and conversation

Text copyright © 2011 J C Jeremy Hobson
Illustrations copyright © 2011 Mandy Shepherd

First published in the UK in 2011
by Quiller, an imprint of Quiller Publishing Ltd
reprinted 2015

British Library Cataloguing-in-Publication Data
A catalogue record for this book
is available from the British Library

ISBN 978 1 84689 092 5

Photographs by Elliot Hobson and the author
unless otherwise credited

Designed by Andrew Barron

Printed in China

### QUILLER

An imprint of Quiller Publishing Ltd
Wykey House, Wykey, Shrewsbury SY4 1JA
Tel: 01939 261616 Fax: 01939 261606
E-mail: info@quillerbooks.com
Website: www.countrybooksdirect.com

# Contents

## Acknowledgements

I must begin by thanking three members of my family without whose help this book would not have been possible. First and foremost, my sister-in-law Mandy Shepherd has provided the superb vignettes which so beautifully illustrate these pages. Photographs have come from numerous sources, all of which have been acknowledged alongside the relevant illustration, but whilst I am extremely grateful to all who took the time and trouble to supply them, I must specifically mention those contributed by my 'new' son, Elliot Hobson. Equally as importantly, my daughter Francesca Geary has given me invaluable help, particularly by making the initial contacts with sporting estates around the UK. Being far more tenacious than I, she achieved results of which I could only ever have dreamed!

In additon, thanks to the country writer and archivist and historian for the National Gamekeepers' Organisation, David S.D. Jones, who has been incredibly supportive of this project. He has supplied me with a great deal of historical text information as well as being kind enough to grant usage of some truly evocative photographs from his private collection.

The sources of recipes are many and varied. Those I would particularly like to thank include: Jane Badcock; Jill Knowles; Steve Reynolds; Nick Pyle; Sarah Rant; the late Tom and Mary Chambers; Jenny Chambers (no relation to Tom and Mary!); Michelle Butterworth; James Benson; Gabriella Manchester; Elizabeth Ainley; Ludovic Barbier; Rosie Graham and Emma Gawlick at Eastnor Castle. The recipe for Crunchy Top Lemon Cake (page 153) came from *Mary Berry's Ultimate Cake Book* published by BBC Books and is reprinted by permission of the Random House Group Ltd.

Researching the chapter, Wine, Coffee and Cigars was, as might be imagined, a very pleasurable experience and resulted in some fascinating material: Simon Chase, non-executive director and consultant to Hunters & Frankau (the UK's sole importer and distributor of the finest Cuban cigars) along with chairman David Lewis, generously provided all the material relating to the après-shoot-lunch cigar; Vicky Williams, PR manager for Berry Bros & Rudd, Britain's oldest wine and spirit merchants, very kindly made suggestions for lunchtime wines and also gave permission for me to use information from their website about The King's Ginger liqueur; Alison and Robert Armes, of Rosie & Java Tea and Coffee Merchant, Richmond-upon-Thames, shared their knowledge and advice relating to lunchtime coffees and the teas best drunk in the afternoon after a hard day on the shoot. Nicholas Radclyffe, owner of the Foxdenton Estate Company, made me realise just how little I knew when it came to the subject of sloe gin and the all-important matters of mid-morning drinks and hip flask fillers! I am grateful to all of these people for their advice and very prompt responses to my requests.

Many old friendships were renewed and new contacts established during the course of researching this book, all of whom offered invaluable help and great kindness in one way or another. They include Monica Dann; Richard Faulks; Colin Barker; David Hudson; Tony Moss; Charles Sainsbury-Plaice at Agripix Ltd: Steve Chesnutt; Frances Atkins; Andrew Duncan; David Knowles, formerly south-east director for the BASC; Jeffrey Olstead, Editor of *Shooting and Conservation* – the official publication of the BASC; Simon Russell-Marsh; Kate Bowles; Malcolm Partridge; Amanda and Christopher Bunbury; James Chapel, director of William Powell Sporting; Tony Ross of Monarchsport (Scotland) Ltd; Cara Richardson; Shaun Trenchard; Kevin Waynn McDermott of Waynnson Gundogs; Mick Jackson and Toby Lawson of the Monckton Shooting Grounds; David Littlewood; Terry Hansom of Hansom Sporting; Mike and Gilly Davies; Nicola Swift of Forman & Field; Evie Good and Jennifer Jordan of the Yadkin Valley Hounds, North Carolina. Others who gave their take on what to look for in a shooting lunch and to whom I am enormously grateful include: Frank Boddy at Ripley Castle; Felicity Cunliffe-Lister (Lady Masham), at Swinton Castle; Alick Barnes of Loyton Lodge; Philip Burtt; Alistair Brew; Peter Willis; William (Will) Garfit; Martin Crosland; William Asprey (from an interview in *Fieldsports* magazine); Colin Corlett; Robert Gibbons (from an article in *The Field*); James Kelly; The Hon Charles Pearson and George, Marquess of Milford Haven (whom I must also thank for allowing photographs to be taken on his West Sussex estate).

The various references to the Linkenholt Estate are the result of an article by Katie Mahon which was published in *Country Illustrated with Hunting Magazine* in 1997 and thanks must be given to the editor, Julie Spencer, and to the author for permission to quote from it.

In the 1980s and 1990s, David & Charles were arguably the foremost publishers of books relating to the countryside in general and field sports in particular. As a result, I have utilised material published by them in Brian Martin's books, *The Big Shoots* and *Tales of the Old Gamekeepers*, and also *The Complete Game Shoot* compiled by John Humphreys. In addition, they were kind enough to allow the quotes from *The Moorland Gamekeeper* by J. Spottiswoode. My grateful thanks to Deborah Jackson for granting formal written copyright permission. Likewise, to Catherine Trippett, permissions manager at the Random House Group for various aspects of help and advice; managing director Roland Philipps also gave his blessing to the inclusion of references to three book titles published by John Murray, namely *No Voice from the Hall* by John Harris, *A Childhood in Scotland* by Christian Miller and *Up and Down Stairs* by Jeremy Musson. Jo Bryant at Debrett's gave permission to include references to *The Big Shots: Edwardian Shooting Parties* and *The Influence of the Chase on Sporting Art and Scenery,* as well as the opportunity to use 'a couple of short extracts'. Charlie Pirie, author of *The Gamekeeper – A Year in the Glen*, was kind enough to write and grant me permission to use the various short quotes from his book and I much appreciate his generosity and best wishes. Permission to quote from *Glen Tanar: Valley of*

*Echoes and Hidden Treasures* by Pierre Fouin was also granted by the author.

Whilst every effort has been made to contact all copyright owners, attempts to trace Webb & Bower, publishers of Wynford Vaughan-Thomas's book *The Countryside Companion*, published in 1979 by Hutchinson/Webb & Bower, were unsuccessful. Efforts were also made to find the copyright owners of material contained within *The Country Book* edited by Barbara Hargreaves and published in 1971 by Countrywise Books; Geoffrey Bles Ltd – the publishers of J. K. Stanford's *The Wandering Gun* (1960) and Elm Tree Books in respect of Shelia Hutchins's *Pâtés & Terrines* (1978). In addition, I have, as far as possible, obtained permission to include any material – no matter how few words – directly quoted from other book or magazine sources or the internet. If I have unintentionally omitted anyone, I can only apologise and request that those affected contact the publishers in order that amends may be made in future reprints.

J C Jeremy Hobson

# Introduction

Shoot lunches are an integral and important part of the day's sport. Their significance is not only to do with staving off the pangs of hunger – although that can be pretty crucial when you have tramped miles in search of the odd cock pheasant – but also with enjoying the camaraderie of like-minded sportsmen and women. No matter whether the shoot is a formal one where lunch is a sit-down affair in a warm cosy lodge or nothing more than a packet of sandwiches eaten in a draughty barn as part of a rough shooting day, any sort of meal-break provides an opportunity to meet new people, re-establish old acquaintances and certainly to indulge in some good-natured badinage. For some, it might also be a chance to get the low-down on some inside knowledge, whether relating to the City, or simply to the discovery that a local gundog breeder has a litter of puppies for sale, or that a nearby farmer

**OPPOSITE TOP** TABLES SET FOR THE SHOOT LUNCH MAY RIVAL THOSE OF THE BEST RESTAURANTS OR...
**BELOW** ...MERELY PROVIDE A BASE ON WHICH TO PLACE SANDWICH BOXES AND THERMOS FLASKS!

has a hedge full of rabbits and is looking for someone to do some ferreting. Jungle drums work well in the countryside and resound even more clearly when accompanied by food and drink.

Even the relatively new phenomenon of simulated game shooting – which offers the opportunity for guests to experience all the excitement of a big-bag driven shoot by the use of clays – is rarely considered without the inclusion of a shooting lunch. At Sunnybanks, on the Stalisfield shoot in Kent, the day starts with bacon butties and coffee at the Wagon and Horses. Halfway through the morning a nip of sloe gin or cherry brandy is taken prior to the two 'drives' before lunch – which is a 'traditional shooting lunch with game and chicken pie, sandwiches, sausages, pasties, sausage rolls [and] soup. Tea and coffee is provided [along] with a selection of wines, beers, port and spirits'.

Interestingly, Queen Victoria refused to condone shooting after lunch and, at Windsor, where this custom was first observed during Prince Albert's time, it was continued until she died, in remembrance of her beloved husband. It was, however, the exception rather than the rule. Nowadays some shoots, no matter what their size, snub the idea of a break of any description in the middle of the day – especially in December when daylight hours are at a premium. Instead they confine themselves to the shortest of mid-morning breaks before shooting through until early afternoon, when pheasants can then be left to roost undisturbed. A long leisurely lunch can then be enjoyed at the end of the day. There is, by the way, much merit in this as far as shooting ethics are concerned, but there is also the fact that, because there is no more sport to be enjoyed, guest Guns are somewhat reluctant to leave! As a well known shooting host recently said after his newly appointed keeper had tried to persuade him to shoot through on a day which promised to be dreary weather-wise and subsequently dark very early: 'No…definitely not. I tried that once before: none of the Guns wanted to go home; they all availed themselves of my wine cellar and I ended up having to give six of the eight guests beds for the night – all of whom insisted on breakfast the next morning, and one of whom didn't actually leave until two days later!'

James Kelly, who oversees the North Glenbuchat Estate in Scotland, cites another, far more practical consideration: 'If you've got guest Guns staying overnight, it just doesn't make sense to shoot through, give them a good lunch late afternoon and then expect them to do justice to a fine dinner at eight pm. Far better to have an early lunch, do a couple of drives afterwards and then finish with a cup of tea and a piece of cake. Guests can then go to their rooms for a shower and a nap and come back down for drinks half an hour or so prior to dinner being served.'

William Asprey, chairman of William & Son, says that, given a choice, he would prefer to break for lunch because 'if you shoot through some of the Guns disappear straight after the shoot and skip lunch, so it is not such a social occasion'.

## PRACTICALITIES AND CHOICE

Some shoots tailor their shooting lunch arrangements according to the time of the season. At Ripley Castle, North Yorkshire, for example, lunch may be taken at either the Boar's Head Hotel or the Hob Green Hotel. However, between September and early November, an al fresco barbeque lunch is offered in the garden of a local cottage, reminding many Guns of a day's partridge shooting in Spain. Once the clocks change, the estate tends to shoot through and the midday meal is replaced by a late lunch at the end of the day's sport. Participating in their noted walk-and-stand days, Ripley's clients are normally expected to bring their own packed lunch, which is then eaten back at the shoot yard at noon. On nearby Hardcastle Moor, Guns are treated to quite a banquet in the recently renovated shoot box. Typical menus might include a cold salad platter of fish, followed by a selection of cold meats, dessert, cheese and fruit and coffee.

For a real gastronomic treat on a lowground estate, how good must it have been to have been invited to the shoot at Linkenholt, Hampshire, in the days when it was run by Christopher Bunbury and his wife Amanda? Both being particularly interested in food, their guests were treated to mid-morning soups that might well have included woodcock stock and beetroot; fried quail's eggs on garlic croutons to accompany the pre-prandial drinks and main courses of perhaps stuffed noisettes of lamb, chicken, leek and ham pie or even, as an antidote to traditional post-Christmas fare, paella served with a white Spanish Rioja. Puddings ranged from blackberry and apple pie to sticky toffee pudding served with a fresh sauce and a bowl of fromage frais. Unfortunately, it seems that an invitation that covers both edible delights and high-class sporting pheasants at Linkenholt is never likely to come my way as, in 2009, not only the shoot, but also the whole village was sold. Fortunately for the private syndicate that shoots there, the shooting rights are leased until February 2013.

At the Langley Wood shoot in Wiltshire, David Kenyon (who is, as he describes it, 'in his day job' the Area Director for England and Wales of the British Deer Society) hosts shooting parties and lunches in the old Edwardian style, but at Newlands in Dumfriesshire, whilst Andrew Duncan's shooting guests are treated to drinks in the drawing-room followed by a lunch of main course, cheese and fruit, Andrew thinks that 'the trend of having more and more elaborate lunches, whether in the middle of the day or at the end, is quite unnecessary'. He goes on to say, 'perhaps [it has an] appeal to those who know nothing if anything about a proper day's shooting and are perhaps more used to expense-account expenses! I am sure that there are some who enjoy this, but it is not for us, who try to treat all our paying visitors as we would our own friends and relations when we have our private days.'

Commercial shoots have undoubtedly had a bearing on how the shooting lunch is seen by Guns who are paying handsomely for their sport. As an invited guest of the shoot owner or captain, almost anyone would be grateful for the sporting opportunities offered and if lunch was a little spartan or even non-existent, then so be it. It is, however, different for the paying guests who quite rightly expect their lunch to be a pleasant, reasonably leisurely occasion served in warm surroundings. On the basis that the customer is always right, it is up to the organisers of the shoot to arrange things so that the client goes away not only talking of the high-flying birds that came his way, but also of the delights of the dining table. It is, in a way, a little like the person who has bought the day playing host to his own dinner party and they should, therefore, be given the opportunity to make it into a social occasion – providing, of course, that it does not affect the remainder of the day's activities.

Sometimes though, 'the tail wags the dog' and one gamekeeper with whom I spoke told me of the quirks of some of his estate's clients throughout the years. 'We've had them all here: we've had people asking for a "Chinese" for lunch – which was made in the kitchens of the house – and one time we even had a request for a mobile fish and chip shop to be brought in, which we did!'

## *Pub grub*

At the other end of the scale, there is the DIY shoot – a phenomenon that has evolved over the last 50 years or so whereby, as John Humphreys describes it in *The Complete Game Shoot* (David & Charles 1992) '… a team of enthusiasts rented and improved their own ground, carrying out rearing and vermin control, and organising the whole shoot themselves in their spare time. They would have no keeper as such but might employ someone part-time to feed or trap… Such a shoot is run for the members and their personal guests and with no commercial pressures.' In an effort to keep those costs down as much as possible, lunch in this situation might therefore be a simple sandwich or a meal taken at the local pub by prior arrangement (and hopefully, at a discount for numbers and regular attendance throughout the season) with the landlord.

Fortunately, pubs feature frequently as venues for the shooting lunch. I say 'fortunately' because such an arrangement not only brings in welcome revenue to a quiet sequestered inn, but also because of the good relations it can engender between the local shoot and the village community. Charlotte Reather, regular columnist for *The Field*, once described her favourite type of shooting meal as being a 'lash lunch' held down at the local once the day's sport is finished: where 'man-pies' and copious amounts of drink are consumed, accompanied perhaps by an impromptu prize-giving of bottles of port for the smallest of reasons – best/worst shot of the day, best dog-handler, and so on.

## *A hut in the wood*

Somewhere in between, there is the type of lunch-break taken in some degree of comfort but yet still technically outdoors. There are plenty of shoots that have an outbuilding (often wooden) erected in some quiet corner of the estate free from vandals and would-be arsonists. Even then there is variety, as author Barbara Hargreaves noted back in 1971:

'Shooting lunches tend to divide themselves roughly into two classes. The pocket pack put together by absent wives, and the cornucopia-like box, carton or basket brought in by wives-in-attendance. The husbands have to bear the weight of these more generous-sized boxes from boot to barn, but the look of envy they receive from those with mere haversack rations must ease the burden considerably... The picnic lunch brought by my sister wives is so far ahead of mine in originality and bulk that, even as I scorn picnic swankery, I make plans to do better next time.

'How can one, after all, compete with someone who brings a picnic in an enormous waste-paper basket? It really looked lovely all lined with a check tablecloth. She only needed to ask her husband to carry it on a stick over his shoulder to complete the Whittington touch. Or with another who flourishes a flask at the assembled company and asks who would care to join them in a ginger-and-rum cocktail?'

Mention is made later in this book of the historical class divide between Guns and beaters, but it is perhaps during the lunch break where a little bit still remains. I have been in woodland shooting huts where the Guns and beaters were separated by nothing more than a wall of straw bales or even, in one case in Surrey, a curtain of plastic: on one side of the curtain the shooting team consumed hot pies, soup and champagne supplied by the host whilst the beaters and pickers-up made do with sandwiches and flasks of coffee brought by themselves. But it was ever thus: talk to gamekeepers of the 'old school' and much is said of the fact that Guns and beaters never mixed – especially not at lunchtime. Brian Martin, in his book *Tales of the Old Gamekeepers* (David & Charles, 1989) mentioned when talking of Bill Gill, keeper at the Wintershall Estate, Surrey: '... that lunch was always an important consideration and taken at a regular time. The keepers and beaters went to a special lunch hut, where they dined well on a big joint of beef or leg of bacon plus bread and cheese, all provided by the estate. There was also a big tub of beer, a wooden barrel, and everyone helped themselves. Meanwhile, the Guns – a traditional mix of local guests and business contacts – went to the big house for more refined fare.'

However, at a shoot I visited in Scotland, some sort of hierarchical compromise seems to have been introduced. Everyone eats together from the same menu but at one end of the outbuilding there is a wood-burning stove and at the other, the door. In between these two points is a long trestle table. Guns have their lunch at the end nearest the fire; next come the old-established beaters and shoot helpers, and then, right by the door, sit newcomers, part-timers and youngsters!

## *On the hill*

Seventy years ago, the father of Pierre Fourin was working as a butler on the Glen Tanar estate near Balmoral and devised a simple yet ingenious method of signalling to his young son that there were leftovers to be had after the grouse-shooting Guns had eaten. 'My lasting memory is of my mother and myself being taken to the foot of the hut road in the estate bus carrying the beaters and dropped off to hide in the heather. After the Guns had lunched, my father would stand at the bothy door and wave a white towel to let us know to walk up and partake of all that had been left. Paté de foie gras and cold grouse washed down with bottles of ginger beer seemed like paradise to a four-year-old...'

Sometimes there is no choice as to a lunchtime venue and it is neither possible nor desirable to move away elsewhere in order to eat, especially in the Highlands where ponies have, for a long time, been the only practical way of getting lunch to the Guns and shot grouse back to the lodge. As Charlie Pirie, gamekeeper and head stalker at Glen Tilt remarked, 'I think it is terrific, after a morning's sport, to see a pony with panniers

A PICNIC FROM A HAMPER WAS, AND IS, SOMETIMES THE ONLY PRACTICAL SOLUTION
OUT ON THE GROUSE MOORS (COURTESY OF D. S. D. JONES)

appear on the skyline in the distance and begin to make its way towards you. You know it's the middle of the day, everyone is ready for lunch, and some of the lads are looking forward to a can of beer or a dram. It's great to see the pony and pony-man come over the brow of the hill – maybe he is still half-an-hour away, but you know he is coming straight for the butts.'

What might be in those panniers is anybody's guess, but a description of lunch transported in this way on one particular Highland shooting estate suggests that they could contain any or all of the following: 'Cold game, ham, beef, chicken, hot lamb stew, pastries, baked potatoes, salads, biscuits, fruit cakes – everything being laid out on white tablecloths spread over the ground. Deer-horn drinking cups… filled with beer and cider and lemonade.' And afterwards: 'With his head resting on a half-empty cartridge bag, the eldest member of the party… snoozes peacefully, a half-finished glass of port tilting in torpid fingers.' (Taken from *A Childhood in Scotland* by Christian Miller.)

## *Sport abroad*

The shoot lunch is no less important when one travels abroad for one's sport. At Estancia Los Chañares (claimed by its owners to be 'the best dove-hunting lodge in Argentina'), breakfast is either taken in an interior dining-room or sometimes outside on the covered terrace. Lunches and dinners (both of which are three courses) are also eaten on the terrace, which contains two open fires for the cooler winter months, whilst the large leather-seated gun room is the focal point for post-shooting and pre- and post-dinner drinks.

At Las Golondrinas, a partridge-shooting estate in south-eastern Spain, the midday lunch break is taken in the field and consists of a selection of traditional Spanish tapas. In Pakistan, a day's shooting might commence with a full breakfast that, typically, includes cereal, milk, eggs, bread, paratha (chapati), jam, honey and cornflakes. Their shooting lunches consist of at least three main courses which, to cater for European tastes, are generally supplemented with crackers, cheese, nuts, fruit, juice, fish, salad, bread and tea or coffee. Guns considering visiting Pakistan will no doubt be somewhat reassured to learn that 'all our cooks and support staff are thoroughly trained in kitchen and table hygiene and observe a strict hygienic code'. I was also much amused to read that on some shooting expeditions there you can 'give your personal water bottles to our kitchen staff every night and they will fill them up with boiling water… which will not only warm you up in your sleeping bags for a sound sleep, but also provide you with safe boiled drinking water for the following day's walk'.

So you see, shooting lunches can be all things to all people. I sincerely hope that this book interests, informs and amuses anyone who enjoys a day's sport with dog and gun – whether it be as a provider of such meals or simply as a consumer!

# A Brief History of the
# Shoot Lunch

Seemingly, not much importance was attached to the subject of lunch in the days when shooting consisted of game being walked-up and shot over moorlands and fields by sportsmen assisted by their pointer and setter dogs. Indeed, in the early part of the 1800s, it was rare for shooting to continue all day and when it did, presumably a late start following a huge breakfast would have sufficed until a cold collation of meats, cheese, bread and beer was taken 'on the hoof' at whatever point was thought most suitable. Things were changing rapidly by the 1860s however; for not only did game begin to be driven towards the Guns by gamekeepers and their teams of beaters, but shooting became a far more social and serious occupation. It is fascinating to compare the comment made in his game book by Mr T. Thornhill, owner of Riddleworth Hall, Norfolk in 1814 where he states, 'Today we killed ninety-

OPPOSITE TOP LOADERS AND GUNS TAKE LUNCH ON RAMSGILL MOOR IN 1934
(COURTESY OF D. S. D. JONES)
BELOW LEFT A.H.B'S PERSONAL BAG – WITH ITS NOTABLE CONTENTS!
BELOW RIGHT BEHIND NORE FOLLY ON THE SLINDON ESTATE, WEST SUSSEX; ONCE STOOD A
THATCHED SHOOTING HUT. SADLY, AS IS THE CASE WITH SO MANY PLACES WHERE LUNCH WAS
ENJOYED, IT HAS BEEN LOST FOREVER.

nine cock pheasants, a feat never before performed in Norfolk, and not likely to be done again', with the bags of quite literally thousands of birds killed at Sandringham and elsewhere in the county less than a century later.

The increased interest in shooting also coincided with a regular and efficient train network and, although steam engines had been transporting goods and people for some considerable time, it was not until around this period that railway carriages were more comfortably furnished and adequately heated. This made the prospect of a trip from London to the grouse moors of northern England and Scotland a far more enticing and practical proposition. Indeed, so popular did grouse shooting become that wealthy sportsmen, their families and domestic staff would migrate by train *en masse*, taking with them every conceivable home comfort plus their gundogs and shotguns. Such travelling was not, however, without mishap and at one time servants were given the carriage nearest the engine because that was the one most likely to suffer in the event of an accident! Gundogs too might fare badly in the most unexpected of ways and author Ivor Smullen recalls an account whereby in 1886, a Mr Alexander Dixon attempted to sue the Great Northern Railway company at Northumberland County Court for damage caused to the tail of his sporting dog:

> '[The dog] travelled safely for a fare of 6s. from King's Cross to Newcastle. But hardly had the dog set foot on the platform when a porter wheeled a truck over its tail. As a result of the injury, the dog, it was stated, could no longer work. Valuing the animal at £60, the judge assessed damages at £25, saying that the accident had happened through the porter's negligence. This decision was reversed by the Divisional Court but their judgement was in turn reversed by the Court of Appeal, a happy decision for Mr Dixon, even if his dog was unable to signal approval in the usual way.'

Accidents notwithstanding, hundreds of sportsmen made the journey to the grouse moor each August but, during the same period, the low-ground estates were not neglected either. As Michael Billett notes in *A History of English Country Sports*, 'The planting of extensive coverts was undertaken… at great expense.' Pheasants and partridges began to be reared; either by catching up birds at the end of the season and hatching the subsequent eggs under broody bantams and chickens, or by the far more complicated Euston System of removing the eggs from any wild bird nests found, substituting 'dummy' eggs and placing the real ones under broody hens. The domestic hens would then sit until the pheasant (or more usually partridge) eggs were just about to chip; at which point they would then be returned to their rightful mother who would, predators permitting, still be sitting the dummy eggs. Eventually, of course, the broody hens would be replaced by incubators but whatever the system used, all this care and attention meant that there was now more game than ever on a gentleman's sporting estate and hosts began organising huge house parties in order to entertain their guests.

It was perhaps King Edward VII who caused formal shoots, big bags and even bigger house parties to become so much in vogue – where he and subsequently, his second son the Prince of Wales (later George V) led, others followed, and shooting etiquette and protocol was undoubtedly influenced by their patronage. Of the various Royal residences, it was to Sandringham that everyone wished to be invited and if there was little chance of being so blessed, at least you could emulate its workings at your very own country retreat.

Traditionally, the sport would be organised over several days and guests were either invited for the duration or for just a part of it. Today, hosts will usually only ever ask the requisite number of Guns (generally seven or eight – although it is not unknown for a generous host to flippantly invite all around a dinner table, especially late at night). In Edwardian times, the owners of some country houses would invite a huge gathering, including a retinue of guest staff such as lady's maids, valets and dog-handlers, and it was possibly not until the evening before a shoot that a guest would learn whether or not he had been successful in gaining a place in the line for the next day. Hopefully everybody's turn would come before the week was out.

## SOMEWHERE TO DINE

Lunch was obviously an essential part of the proceedings and was taken in all manner of places. On some estates, a marquee was erected, whilst on others, a table was set out in the open, and the Guns were attended to by the household butler and footmen. On a grouse moor, lunch was often served in a specially constructed shooting 'box', which, although somewhat primitive to look at from the outside, nevertheless permitted a meal to be served in the greatest of comfort. Food was transported by horse and cart (of which more later) and was either made at the 'Big House', or prepared at a nearby hostelry – as was the case at Ramsgill, Nidderdale, North Yorkshire, where the Yorke Arms provided whatever sustenance was required. (Unfortunately Frances Atkins, who is currently at the Yorke Arms, has no record of the actual foodstuffs that might once have been supplied.)

At nearby Hardcastle Moor, there is also a purpose-built shooting box that was built in the 1850s. In 2005, not only was the roof replaced, but the main dining area was extended. A little while later, things were improved even further and there are now washing and toilet facilities – which are apparently much appreciated, particularly by the lady guests. In his book *The Moorland Gamekeeper*, J Spottiswoode described his impressions of the shooting huts on the Knarsdale moors when he first went beating there not long after the end of the First World War:

EATON LODGE WAS BUILT PRIMARILY AS A LUNCH VENUE BY
THE 1ST DUKE OF WESTMINSTER. (COURTESY OF D. S. D. JONES)

'Each beat had an identical lunch hut of quite a large size, with two compartments, one for the Guns and one for the keepers, beaters and other attendants at the shoot. The latter had bench seats all round and was really comfortable. Each structure was built of wood, with a felted roof, and was entirely waterproof. Each hut was sited in a sheltered hollow near a hill burn, and very convenient for the line of butts used before lunch and for those to be occupied immediately after. There was no real road to any of these huts. The old man, with his equally old horse and cart, who carried out the lunch had to pick his way over the sounder parts of the moor after leaving the Ward Way – a long narrow green lane along which the farmers drove their sheep to and from their respective hill grazings.'

Writing in *Shooting*, a book published in 1903 as part of the Country Life Library of Sport, editor and contributor Horace G. Hutchinson was clearly enthused by the design of a rustic, heather-covered shooting hut on the Glenmuick moor which was owned at the time by Sir Allan Mackenzie:

'Not the least ingenious part of the whole arrangement is the door, which is a square of the size of the front wall's height – I mean, that is of equal height with the wall, and is just about as broad as it is high. It works on hinges from the lower beam of the roof, the beam that runs along the top of the wall. It opens outwards, and outside the hut, at the distance of the door's length from it, is a wooden frame of two uprights and a horizontal just the height of the door. There are two hooks on the horizontal, corresponding to two loops on the door, so that when the hooks are fastened in the loops the door is supported horizontally, allowing light to come into the hut, and forming a kind of verandah roof for keeping out the rain. The whole thing is ingeniously simple and picturesque, and infinitely better than those corrugated-iron-roofed abominations that we sometimes see put up as shelters on the moor.'

King Edward VII had a lunch-room built as an extension to the railway station at Wolferton for the times he was in residence at Sandringham and was shooting nearby. Meanwhile in Cheshire, a mock Tudor lodge was built on the Eaton Estate in the late nineteenth century, primarily as a luncheon venue, by the first Duke of Westminster. According to David S. D. Jones, country writer, archivist and historian for the National Gamekeepers Organisation, whose relatives lived there during the early 1900s and visited on a regular basis during the 1940s and 1950s, it 'was built around a large dining-room, equipped with expensive furniture, paintings and silver cutlery [it was] used by the Westminsters for luncheon purposes whenever they were shooting in the vicinity of Eaton Park. On these occasions, food and drink was brought out from Eaton Hall and the butler and footmen waited on the guests.'

Shooting lodges were often every bit as important a building as the main house – in fact, at Garrowby, North Yorkshire, what is now The Hall started life as a shooting box but was subsequently extended. Elsewhere, lodges where shooting parties gathered and lunch was consumed have sadly either been lost forever or been subject to change: many are now private homes or even, as in the case of Grinton Lodge – situated in the Yorkshire Dales National Park – turned into a youth hostel run by the YHA. At Slindon, West Sussex, the National Trust owns Nore Folly, a strangely shaped edifice which, depending on whether you are of a romantic or practical engineering mind, resembles either the portcullis entrance to a medieval castle or a railway tunnel. Although the folly (as with all such buildings) was never intended to serve any practical purpose and was constructed in the mid-eighteenth century on the instructions of Barbara, the Countess of Newburgh, behind it there was once a thatched luncheon hut where owners of the Slindon Estate refreshed themselves and their guests while out shooting. Unfortunately, although the folly itself still stands proudly at the edge of a pheasant covert and overlooks game crops and prime shooting ground, of the thatched lodge itself, there is no sign at all.

Purely as a piece of social history, it is interesting to note that the selling off or demolition of some lodges (and indeed many country houses) came about as a result of a general farming depression which reached its peak after the Second World War. Most landowners were by then in debt to a lesser or greater degree and, as these debts mounted because agricultural rents were not forthcoming, there was often no alternative but to pull down buildings for which there were no funds to maintain them, or to sell off what was known in land agent's jargon, 'outlying parts' of the estate – often the location of the family shooting lodge.

## A Room in the House

Occasionally, the head gamekeeper's house was requisitioned for use as a suitable venue for shooting lunches. In this case the estate workers would, on the instructions of the landowner, often build an extension, which then became a little like a Sunday parlour. The keeper's children and family would never enter it except for the most formal of events. Things were, however, a little different at Broadlands when it was owned by Earl Mountbatten of Burma, and royal shooting lunches were taken at the home of head keeper Harry Grass. David S. D. Jones recounts how things worked:

'Shortly after Harry and Stella Grass moved to Broadlands in 1959, the head keeper's house at Ridge, Yewtree Cottage, was extensively modernised and upgraded. As part of this refurbishment, the wall between the two rooms at the front of the house was removed and replaced with a set of wooden doors which could be folded away to create a large dining-room for when members of the royal family came to shoot with Lord Mountbatten. At the same time, a cloakroom with a toilet, wash basin and coat hanging facilities was installed adjacent to the room.

'The Grass family had full use of these rooms, but were obliged to remove their furniture (excepting the piano!), prior to a shoot day. On these occasions, staff from Broadlands set up trestle tables, and brought in dining chairs, napery and silver cutlery from the mansion, creating a stylish dining-room for the royal party. Lunch was prepared in the mansion by Mrs Jones, Lord Mountbatten's cook, before being taken out to Yewtree Cottage in an estate car by a footman, who was often accompanied by a couple of non-shooting royal ladies who came to dine with the guns. Hot dishes were re-heated on Stella Grass's Rayburn cooker, prior to being served to the guests by Lord Mountbatten's butler, Charles Smith, at about one o'clock.

'Broadlands shoot lunches were fairly simple affairs, usually consisting of a watery stew or a beef hotpot. The sweet course was normally a steamed pudding. Guests were offered cherry brandy and other liqueurs with the meal – or a non-alcoholic drink. Throughout the duration of the lunch, Stella Grass and her youngest daughter washed up the guests' plates and cutlery. However, before the Guns departed for the first drive of the afternoon, the Queen sent for Stella and thanked her publicly in the dining-room for allowing the use of her home for luncheon purposes.'

Stella Grass was apparently particularly fond of Lady Thomas Sopwith, who always brought a pair of carpet slippers to wear during lunch in order not to dirty the dining-room carpet with her shoes. Male Guns were less formal, taking their boots off outside the house and wandering around in stockinged feet.

Elsewhere though, keeping things neat and tidy and the keeper's family from causing damage was not always easy. Gladys Smart, a housekeeper to a grand family in Norfolk before ending her life as the same to a widower gamekeeper in Yorkshire, once stated that, 'I've been responsible for the dining-room here in the Lodge – and a difficult enough job it is too. Even though it's a part of my home, I have to treat it as if it is not. My terrier Rusty seems to spend his life wanting to get in the room and onto the furniture and Albert's grandchildren find nothing more exciting than charging about in a room I'm paid to keep ready for the shooting party.'

Such impositions were, however, not always inconvenient: Brian Martin, in *Tales of the Old Gamekeepers*, quotes gamekeeper Frank Hunt as saying that, during his time as head keeper to Captain Jolliffe at Ammerdown Park: '... lunch was always held at the head keeper's cottage... and when all the Guns had taken their fill we used to entice them into the sitting-room as quickly as possible, by lighting the fire to make them nice and cosy, so that we could move in and feast on the leftovers!'

## THE CLASS DIVIDE

As for the keepers and beaters, they were lucky if they had a covered area in which to retire at lunchtime. On the moors, they would either eat their 'bait' a respectful distance from the shooting party, or possibly at the house of a nearby hill farmer. Writer Christian Miller spent her childhood on her father's Scottish estate and recalls: 'Discreetly separated

KEEPERS AND LOADERS WOULD ALWAYS EAT A DISCREET DISTANCE AWAY FROM THE GUNS.
(COURTESY OF D. S. D. JONES)

from us by a hillock or a clump of trees, the loaders and dogs shared "doorsteps" – jaw-stretching sandwiches several inches thick, stuffed with homemade cheese or last year's scarlet raspberry jam.'

On a low-ground shoot the beaters would, certainly at the turn of the 1900s, generally shelter in the lee of a covert and line up ready to be served bread, cheese and beer by one of the estate's under-keepers. For a long time, beaters were equipped with smocks that identified them as being a legitimate part of the estate's proceedings – such was the opportunity to obtain a beater's wage and a fairly hefty midday meal that it was not unknown for locals with nothing whatsoever to do with the shoot to try and attach themselves to the party.

In the days of the Bonham Carters (relatives of the actress Helena Bonham Carter) the Buriton Manor estate was recognised as one of the finest shoots in Hampshire and held about eight pheasant shoots each season. Each day required twenty beaters and as many as thirty boys (or girls on some occasions if they couldn't get enough boys) acting as 'stops'. The keeper's sons would apparently deliver a summary of requirements to the village schoolmaster, a Mr Patrick, who would then choose the boys to act as stops. Each of them would be paid 8d (3½p) for the day but would also get a good lunch: two sausages, bread, a mince pie and a drink of tea or coffee. The beaters would get about 2/6d (12½p) for the day and their packed lunch would be followed by beer, usually supplied in four- or five-gallon stone jars encased by a wicker basket.

On every shoot at this time there would almost always be a very obvious class divide. The attitude of some of the Guns of the time to the beaters is illustrated by the comment a 1920s guest on a West Riding estate is reputed to have made to his host: 'The men are quite human; I actually talked to one before luncheon and I could understand what he said.'

A little more enlightened about a decade and a half later, was E.C. Keith, a well-travelled Gun whose main delight was, nevertheless, to shoot partridges in his home county of Norfolk. 'The beaters are also patiently standing by… one we notice leaning on his stick to which is attached a flag… Have five minutes' chat with this man, and he will quickly reveal an interest and an intelligence which his attitude and garb belie. He may have arisen before daylight to feed cattle so as to be free to beat, for he much enjoys the day, the communal lunch and the beer. By his flag we know that he is a flanker and as such a very responsible person.'

Even today, there is often a separation between Guns and shoot helpers when it comes to lunchtime – although that often is as much to do with the practicalities of space as anything else. However, the 'them and us' legacy remains and there is still a certain hierarchy on some shoots: Guns are fed in the dining-room, loaders and visiting keepers in the kitchen (where they usually eat the same food as is being served in the dining-room), and beaters out in the outbuildings (where they may or may not be supplied with warm food, soup, bread rolls and cheese, accompanied by beer and a bottle or two of whisky to share).

## LADIES WHO LUNCHED

The concept of 'ladies who lunch' is not a new one. There has long been a tradition where the wives of shooting guests are driven out to the luncheon venue and then possibly watch the first drive after lunch. Anthony Vandervell and Charles Coles, writing in *Game and the English Landscape* (Debrett's Peerage 1980) had this to say on the possible origins of ladies in the shooting field: 'Victorian ladies joined the scene, sometimes to shoot, but more often to accompany the party. With their recent return to the hunting field this recalled the customs of Elizabethan hawking several hundred years before. The shooting luncheon soon became a part of the day's sport comparable with the large food hampers that had always been taken to the races – unless a substantial meal was to be served in a lodge or marquee.'

Bringing the ladies out to lunch was not necessarily always a joyous occasion: in their book, *The Lost Poems of W. H. Kennings*, authors Valentine Hardy and Philippe de Randolph

INDOORS OR OUT, LADIES OFTEN JOINED THE GUNS FOR LUNCH DURING THE EDWARDIAN PERIOD – AS CAN BE SEEN, THE ABSENCE OF A DINING-ROOM DIDN'T MEAN THAT IT SHOULD BE ANY LESS GRAND AN OCCASION! (COURTESY OF NICK RADCLYFFE)

make mention of the fact that Kenning's mother, Alice, died relatively young in 1911, as the result of a heart attack that occurred whilst out shooting. As the authors note: 'On many estates, it was customary for the ladies to come and join the Guns for an outdoor picnic lunch and the attack, a massive one, happened as she was climbing into the horse-drawn trap in readiness for her return to the house of her host.' Only slightly less alarming is the notion that one might have been hit on the head by a falling pheasant – as was the case with a certain Edwardian, Lady Ailesbury, who took twelve weeks to recover from such an incident.

On today's shoots, you are just as likely to find the ladies out all day – either shooting, picking up or in the beating line. For those who still come out only for the lunch period, the advent of a mid-morning break can mean that they join the shooting party then and watch the pre-lunch drives before either slipping away after the meal or staying on for the rest of the afternoon. It is perhaps worthy of note that they are in good company for, despite her enthusiasm for working her dogs, if one of the royal racehorses was running whilst she was a guest at Broadlands during the 1960s and 1970s, the present Queen would occasionally spend the afternoon in the head keeper's cottage watching a particular race on television, rather than re-joining the Guns on the shooting field!

Sexist though it might seem to record, picking up has always been popular with the mothers and wives of shooting men, especially on the family shoot (girlfriends, particularly new ones, tend to be kept on the peg in order that they can be impressed by the prowess of their hunter-gatherer companion!). Ladies who shot – as opposed to merely lunched – and then gained a taste for picking up in later years, include the likes of Hampshire-based stalwarts such as the late Countess of Brecknock who, with her black labrador Conker, gathered many birds shot by the Guns on her estate at Wherwell. Others, including of course HM The Queen, have been content to surround themselves with a brace or so of labradors and set about their work with quiet efficiency and no particular desire to fire a shotgun. Whilst on the subject of ladies in the shooting field, according to the opinion of Queen Victoria, ' ... only "fast" women shoot'!

◆

## EATING 'AL FRESCO'

Throughout the decades, there have always been shoots where even aristocratic Guns preferred to eschew the dining-room protocol in favour of a few precious extra hours out on the hill or in the field. Lunch, where it was felt to be necessary, came in the form of a hamper brought to a certain place at a previously agreed time (much in the same way as a groom brings a second horse to a particular place on a hunting day). For many, the sport was the main reason for being out and scant attention was paid to the needs of the inner man – as evidenced by George A. B. Dewar writing in 1903: 'I liked to get up occasional shooting parties, comprised of a few farmers and others in the district who could shoot, and who moreover could bring a dog or two; and great fun those jolly, unconventional parties used to be. How we were wont to cut short the luncheon of bread and cheese and beer, and what zest there was in the woodcock shilling sweepstake!'

A short break for a shooting picnic is, therefore, not necessarily a modern thing. In certain parts of Scotland, especially during the Edwardian period, it was considered the norm for the sportsman to go out onto the hill daily, in order to indulge either in stalking, or walked-up grouse shooting, taking with him a gamekeeper or ghillie. At lunchtime, the sportsman would often eat his meal alone whilst the staff sat elsewhere to eat theirs. To illustrate the point, David S.D. Jones (who has, incidentally, written an extensive history of the property) thus describes typical events at Eishken, a 69,000 acre estate on the Isle of Lewis that was at the time leased by Mr and Mrs Joseph Platt:

'Guests at Eishken Lodge woke to the sound of the Platts' keeper-piper, parading up and down in front of the lodge, playing stirring tunes on his bagpipes. While they were breakfasting, ghillies replenished the peats in their bedrooms, ensuring a supply of fuel for evening fires. Towards the end of breakfast, a notebook was passed around, enabling them to order a selection of items for their packed lunch from the daily menu. Typical choices might include venison pie, ham, tongue or local lamb, and a selection of cheeses and cakes, all of which would be packed into an enamelled tin box, with "extras" such as bread and butter or biscuits wrapped in greaseproof paper parcels and tied to the outside. Each guest would be provided with a small flask of whisky to accompany their lunch.

'Apart from on the Sabbath, when a substantial cooked luncheon was served, followed by afternoon tea, sporting guests were expected to eat their packed lunch on the hill, by the loch or on the grouse moor, rather than in the vicinity of the lodge. Non-sporting visitors were encouraged to go for a long walk, whatever the weather, and to take a packed lunch with them. It was an unwritten house rule that all guests did not return to the lodge until after five pm on weekdays, thus allowing the domestic staff to dust and polish throughout the building and to have a short rest during the afternoon.'

## Horses for Courses

Whether there was ever any such rest for the outdoor staff is a moot point. Keepers and ghillies would, of course, be out with their 'gentlemen' and behind them would be a retinue of grooms and stable lads on hand to deal with the ponies, traps and game carts, all of which were essential to the success or otherwise of a shooting day.

In today's shooting society where 4 x 4s are the absolute workhorse, we tend to bundle everything into the available space, knowing that we have wet-weather clothes to hand, a flask (alcoholic or not) in the glove compartment and the horsepower to get from drive to drive and back to the appointed mid-morning or lunchtime rendezvous. Generations ago,

A PACKED LUNCH
EATEN 'AL FRESCO' IS AN OLD
ESTABLISHED TRADITION –
ESPECIALLY ON THE MOORS OF
SCOTLAND AND
NORTHERN ENGLAND
(COURTESY OF DAVID HUDSON)

# At the Start of the Day

Although this book is primarily concerned with the midday or main meal of a shooting day, I couldn't let the start of the day's sport go without a mention. After all, sporting sustenance is not necessarily confined to lunchtime: a shoot breakfast is often a substantial affair. J. G. Bertam wrote in 1889 of a breakfast he ate prior to a day on the hill which included a salmon steak, 'a helping from a pie composed of jellied sheep's head nicely seasoned and palatable', an omelette, scones, oatcakes, marmalade and honey, 'into which liberal spoonfuls of whisky had been added'.

Personally, I love the idea of cold ham and poached eggs for breakfast – an idea which apparently originated in the Middle Ages, but, according to the Reader's Digest *Farmhouse Cookery*, did not become popular until much later: 'It was not until the Victorian era that bacon and eggs appeared

**OPPOSITE TOP** IN SOME RESPECTS, A SHOOTING BREAKFAST MIGHT, IN FACT, BE REMINISCENT OF A HUNT BREAKFAST — AS IS BEING ENJOYED HERE BY MEMBERS OF THE YADKIN VALLEY HOUNDS OF ADVANCE, NORTH CAROLINA (COURTESY OF JENNIFER JORDAN).
**BELOW** MEMENTOES FROM A GLORIOUS PAST LINE THE WALLS OF THIS CLASSIC SHOOT ROOM IN CONVERTED STABLES AT HOLFIELD GRANGE, ESSEX (COURTESY OF ANDREW JOHNSTON).

is of the opinion that 'if breakfast has to bring you round or set you up for the rigours of the day, then no question, devilled kidneys on toast washed down by Black Velvet will put colour back in your cheeks…'

---

*The quantities given here are for eight people.*
48 lamb kidneys
225g/8oz plain flour
4 teaspoons each of cayenne pepper and English mustard powder
115g/4oz butter
4-6 drops of Worcestershire sauce
200ml/7fl oz game or chicken stock
16 slices toast

---

Remove the membrane from the kidneys and slice each in half. In a bowl, mix together the flour, cayenne pepper and mustard powder. Toss the kidneys in the flour/spice mix and shake off any excess. Heat a large frying pan and melt the butter (without letting it burn and brown) and as it melts, add the flour-dusted kidneys, stirring, turning and cooking for approximately five minutes. Add the Worcestershire sauce (more than is shown in the ingredients list if you like) and the stock. Let the combination fuse and meld before sharing out the kidneys (using a slotted spoon) between the slices of toast. Turn up the heat under the frying pan and let the remaining sauce thicken and emulsify; pour over the kidneys and serve immediately.

## Kippers

Love them or hate them, kippers are an interesting possibility. Writer Douglas Tate once declared that whilst a breakfast of almost any kind of locally caught fish would help cure the problems of a 'punishing previous evening', the ultimate restorer is a kippered herring. He stated, 'The kippers should be grilled and served without ornament of any kind save for lashings of coarse brown bread, with perhaps a morsel of butter, to dislodge any fine bones encountered by the too-eager eater.' Like the devilled kidneys mentioned elsewhere in this section, kippers can be washed down with Black Velvet, but it is Douglas's opinion that on Boxing Day, 'champagne is a must.'

## A Continental breakfast

Plates full of mixed cold meats, a selection of soft cheeses, halved hard-boiled eggs and a basketful of brioche slices, croissants, *pain au chocolat* and toasted bread will do the trick. Pots full of good quality coffee just about complete the perfect Continental breakfast – the only problem may be that picking at such delights tends to make guests more and more relaxed and less inclined towards booting up in readiness for the day's sport!

You could enhance further the Continental theme by offering eggs cooked in the following way – but having to cook them, does, I must admit, somewhat take away from having everything on the table and ready to serve before the day's guests arrive.

## Oeufs en Cocotte à la Crème

*You will need eight ovenproof ramekins or similar.*
30g/1oz butter
salt and pepper
8 eggs
8 tablespoons double cream
a few dried chopped mushrooms or fried bacon lardons (optional)

Smear a little butter in the bottom of each ramekin, together with a tiny amount of salt and pepper (you could, if you wish, include a few fried chopped mushrooms or cooked, finely chopped bacon lardons in each). Break an egg into each dish and further season if required. Gently pour a tablespoon of cream over each egg and top off with a little dab of butter. Place the ramekins into a roasting dish and pour around them just enough boiling water for it to come halfway up the outside of the dishes. Place the tin in a pre-heated oven, gas mark 6/200°C and bake for 7–8 minutes or until the whites have just set and the yolks are still runny. Take to the table immediately they are removed from the oven – your guests need to be ready and waiting otherwise the eggs will continue to cook.

## Breakfast in a Bun

There's a lot to be said for hand-held food! It is best to prepare beforehand as many baps (white and wholemeal) as you think might be needed. Cut them in half and have some soft butter readily available, as well as a bottle of tomato ketchup – it is surprising just how many people are closet ketchup lovers! Suggested fillings include cooked rashers of bacon, rings of black pudding and sliced (lengthways) sausages. Keep the food warm on an electric hotplate or in a low oven. Alternatively, offer thin-cut grilled gammon steaks (perhaps even with an accompaniment of warmed pineapple rings). From experience, it is probably best to avoid fried or poached eggs, as these will either congeal whilst waiting to be eaten, or be so runny that they trickle down the wrist just as soon as the first mouthful of the bap is taken. Sliced cooked mushrooms might seem to be a tasty idea but can end up on the floor! If sliced tomatoes are included, ensure that they are thickly cut. Allow guests to help themselves – the alluring smell will ensure that they do.

## Coffee & Biscuits

Whilst now is not the time or place to indulge in the finer aspects of coffee-making, which will be far better appreciated later in the day, even those who are not serving breakfast should have an ample supply in readiness for the first arrivals. It always pays to have a kettle on the boil for those guests who prefer tea (whether ordinary or herbal) as well as a few small bottles of mineral water for those who come in looking like they might have had a late night…

The biscuits you provide could of course come from your local supermarket but you could always make your own if you have time. Biscuits are easy to make and the more uneven the shape, the more homemade they look! Whilst they can be uneven in shape, they should, however, be even in thickness; otherwise, as they cook the thinner ones will be ready before the thicker ones are cooked right through. Remember to place each biscuit well away from its neighbours on the baking tray, as they have a habit of spreading. Generally, in a normal oven (as opposed to fan-assisted), it is best to bake biscuits in the centre, as this helps to give them even baking and colouring.

TERRY AND RUSSELL HANSOM'S SHOOTING GUESTS GATHER FOR MEALS AT
THE OLD RAY ESTATE SAWMILL (COURTESY OF HANSOM SPORTING)

## Ginger Biscuits

*To make about 40*
225g/8oz sugar
125ml/4fl oz golden syrup
125g/4oz margarine
350g/12oz self-raising flour
2 teaspoons ginger
¼ teaspoon cinnamon (optional)
1 level teaspoon bicarbonate of soda
1 beaten egg
a little butter (optional)

Put the sugar, syrup and margarine in a pan and melt over a very low heat. Sift flour, cinnamon and bicarb into a bowl. Mix in the melted ingredients and add the beaten egg. Mix again.

Roll teaspoonfuls of the mixture into little balls and place them well apart on a greased and floured baking tray. Cook at gas mark 4/180°C for about 20 minutes, or until they are golden-brown and slightly 'cracked'. Leave to cool and then turn out onto a wire rack to get hard.

## Crunchy Oat Cookies

Just think of these as being a homemade version of Hobnobs. The ingredients given will make about a dozen huge biscuits – increase the quantities in proportion for more.

75g/3oz porridge oats
55g/2oz plain flour
55g/2oz margarine
55g/2oz granulated sugar
1 level tablespoon golden syrup
½ level teaspoon bicarbonate of soda

Mix together the porridge oats and flour in a bowl. Melt the margarine in a large pan with the sugar and syrup. Gently sprinkle the bicarbonate of soda into the mix and then add the contents of the bowl. Mix and stir well. Make large spoon-shaped (quenelles) balls of the mixture and place them, well apart, on a well greased and floured baking tray. Bake at gas mark 4/180°C for 10–15 minutes. Allow to cool in traditional fashion.

## A Breakfast Meeting

Breakfast is, however, more than just a means of staving off the pangs of hunger prior to the day's exertions and John King, of John King Coaching based in Swindon, says; 'Our shoot days are first and foremost traditional social occasions so naturally we always start with a relaxed, sit-down breakfast. A wholesome English start to set everyone up for the day and to begin the process of the Guns and their guests all getting to know each other.'

A few years ago, a bakery company came up with the idea of a range of dog biscuits that owners could share with their pets. Their publicity department stated that the biscuits, which were given names such as Liver Love and Carob Crunch, were apparently made 'with human quality ingredients [and were] harder than human biscuits to suit dog's teeth'. A newspaper report at the time prompted the following response from a Scottish shooting enthusiast: 'Nothing new in this; methinks. I used to carry some Bonios for my dogs whilst shooting (it stopped them drooling whilst I ate my lunch) and it was quite common for me to nibble at one – to the disgust of my dogs – whilst awaiting the retrieve of a bird. Alas, my beloved caught me... and informed the assembled company ... only to be told by the rest of the Guns that they too enjoyed the occasional Bonio whilst out shooting!'

◆

Terry and Russell Hansom of Hansom Sporting say much the same of any break, no matter at what point of the shooting day it is taken: 'We always have a barbeque at the end of the first day of our syndicate shoots; we feel it helps in introducing new members, together with catching up with old friends…' The Guns meet and eat at the old Ray Estate Sawmill where there is a fitted kitchen, complete with a Calor gas cooker, so that breakfast, early morning coffee, lunch and a pot of tea at the end of the day can all be prepared.

Shooting being the gregarious sport it undoubtedly is, strangers will soon make a point of getting to know one another but even so, making proper introductions and 'meeting and greeting' should be the responsibility of the host or designated shoot captain.

## The Host's Role

The role of shoot captain is an important one – so much so that in his book *The Complete Game Shoot*, writer and sportsman John Humphreys devotes a whole chapter to his duties. Generally, the task is carried out by the host (who normally owns the land or at least has his name on the rental agreement) but occasionally it may be a representative from a sporting letting agency or someone employed specifically to take charge when the boss is away.

One of his most elementary duties is to know where he is going on a particular day and where exactly the gamekeeper has placed the pegs for each drive. There can be nothing more embarrassing than taking a team of Guns into a field or woodland ride and being

**OPPOSITE**
THE DUTIES OF HOST OR SHOOT CAPTAIN CAN, AT TIMES, BE QUITE PLEASURABLE!

unsure as to where the peg for a back-gun has been placed. An hour or two spent going round all the intended drives a day or two before the shooting day is therefore far better than just having a telephone conversation with the keeper the night before. A possible route from drive to drive should also be discussed as the keeper and beating line will not be best pleased to discover a line of 4 x 4 vehicles parked at the end of a spinney down which they are trying to blank birds into more substantial woodland. Also, as John Humphreys states: 'It is likely that the shoot layout will be familiar to both the keeper and shoot captain, so the drives may not take long to plan; but if the weather appears set to ruin it and you reverse drives, are you *certain* that there is a plank across that wide ditch?'

## Meeting and greeting

It is the meeting and greeting element that is likely to concern us most at the beginning of the day. As host/captain, it is always best to be at the agreed rendezvous long before the first guest is expected: the time is never wasted because not only can any overnight changes be discussed with the keeper, there are other, seemingly inconsequential jobs to be done such as making sure that the coffee machine is on, mugs, milk and sugar laid out and a plate of biscuits set out in readiness for the first arrivals. It is the little things that will make the Guns feel welcome. It is also worth checking with whoever is responsible for providing the mid-morning nibbles and lunch itself, that times for both have been agreed and that red wine has been brought from wherever it is kept and white wine been placed to chill. (I know from experience that offering a glass as the Guns come in at lunchtime and then realising the bottles are not where they should be, can cause unnecessary stress!)

Guest Guns not previously known to you will introduce themselves on arrival, and then it is your job to remember their names so that you can introduce them to their fellow Guns as they arrive: if, like me, you are good with faces but not with names, this is not always as easy as it sounds. As general conversation-opening gambits, you can never go wrong by asking if the guest has much shooting planned for the season, but a shooting host I know always gets himself out of any deathly silence by asking 'What's the most interesting thing that's happened to you this week?' To my way of thinking, the question could open a whole unwanted can of worms but he claims it always works for him!

With guests I've met before, I always try to remember a conversation from the last time we were together and broach that subject but even that is not without potential disaster: take for instance a casual enquiry about the wonderful young gundog that accompanied the guest on his last visit, only to be told in reply that it had unfortunately been run over the previous week.

OPPOSITE

A FRIENDLY GREETING IS THE BEST INTRODUCTION

## *Drawing for numbers*

Conversational *faux pas* notwithstanding, once everyone has arrived it is time to draw for peg numbers. This is, surprisingly, not that old a tradition and at the turn of the last century or just before, it was quite normal for Guns to be placed by their host. In his book *Sport*, W. Bromley-Davenport described what was apparently common practice in 1885: 'Hazel slips stuck in the ground about eighty or a hundred yards from the covert, with a small piece of paper in a cleft at the top, mark the positions of the four forward guns whom the host places before taking himself off with the others to walk in line with the beaters.'

Nowadays, the drawing of numbers and the subsequent moving up by two or three places after each drive appears to be the norm. Position finders can be numbers on the bottom of small shot glasses (found only after the contents have been drunk) or markers made from plastic or ivory and kept in a small leather wallet. Many hosts use playing cards – George Milford Haven is one such person, as he claims to have been given and then lost so many proper marker sets that he finds the playing card option to be far better and infinitely cheaper! Nick Radclyffe, owner of the Foxdenton Estate Company Ltd (which is also the purveyor of the most wonderful sloe gin, more details of which can be found on page 66),

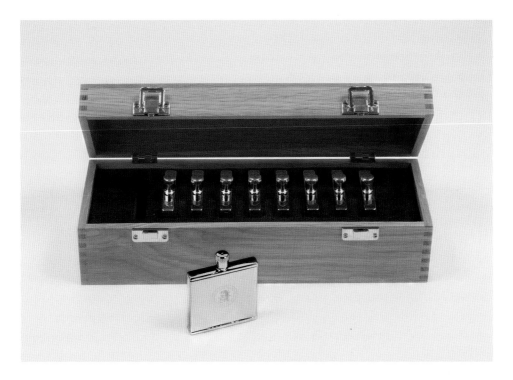

FOXDENTON ESTATE COMPANY CAN PROVIDE AN INTERESTING SET OF PEG NUMBERS!
(COURTESY OF NICK RADCLYFFE)

can supply a boxed set of mini hip flasks, each of which is numbered one to nine. Arranged in the box so that the engraved numbers on their sides cannot be seen, they are perhaps the most unique (and potentially most enjoyable) way of drawing for numbers I have ever seen!

After peg numbers have been drawn, the host or shoot captain must give the pre-shoot talk, especially important in these careful days of health and safety. This should include what may or may not be shot, and when – some shoots, for example, have a policy of not shooting at a pigeon until the first pheasant has been seen – and it should be emphasised that there is to be no shooting once the horn or whistle signifying the end of the drive has been blown. Other items of note, such as the fact that spent cartridges must be collected/left by the peg, or that there are to be two drives before the mid-morning break, two after, and a final two after lunch will all help to ensure that the guests enjoy their day more thoroughly.

## On Being the Perfect Guest

In complete contrast to the worries of the host, it is a relatively simple matter to be the perfect guest. If the 'call to arms' arrives as a formal written invitation, then it is important to be prompt in responding – any tardiness may result in the host thinking that you are not interested and offering the place to someone else. If, on the other hand, one cannot accept the invitation, a polite letter of regret will almost certainly result in an alternative day being offered: it will probably be later in the season but the possible lack of birds will most likely be recompensed by their quality. Once the invitation has been accepted, only the most severe of crises should prevent you from attending – Granny dying for the umpteenth time in her life is not much of an excuse, especially when it is given because of subsequently receiving a better offer!

Satellite navigation has lessened the worry of getting lost when searching for an unknown shoot, but even so, it will pay to download a map of the area from the internet or to look at a road atlas the night before. Personally, I have a profound fear of arriving anywhere late, so much so that I generally arrive at least half an hour too early and have to park up some distance away from where I'm supposed to be to while away the minutes. Much

Whilst this is not in any way intended to be a book on how to run a shoot, it is worth pointing out that anyone connected with running a day's shooting must be acquainted with current Health and Safety regulations and also have completed a Risk Assessment for the estate. Some basic knowledge of first aid is also desirable and the numbers of the nearest emergency services should be programmed into one's mobile phone.

◆

better to be early than late, though. As Owen Jones wrote in his 1910 book, *Ten Years of Game-Keeping*: 'Some guns are apparently born late. But if it is rude to be late for a dinner party, surely it is rude to be late for a shoot. At a dinner the late guest is the chief sufferer, because he must eat warmed-up food or go without. At a shoot the host and his punctual guests, the keeper, the bag, and the success of the day, all must suffer.'

You may be able to shoot equally as well (or badly) dressed in T-shirt and jeans as you can in a shooting suit, but a sloppy turn-out is an insult to your host and fellow guests. Shooting clothes have evolved for logical reasons: the most obvious being comfort, warmth and movement. There is also the question of personal safety – feet and ankles are better protected on uneven or rough ground by stout boots or specifically designed Wellingtons. Traditionally, one should also wear a tie. Not only does it look smart, in an emergency it could always be used as a makeshift dog lead or, heaven forbid, a tourniquet or arm sling.

Almost every book and article written on the subject of shooting mentions the need for a well-behaved gundog. Why is it then that so many badly trained dogs are seen on the field? There is no pleasure in being accompanied by an animal that runs wild at the end of each drive and squeaks abominably during it – you might get away with this on your own shoot or in a situation where you and your dog are known and tolerated by all, but as a first-time guest on a new shoot, your dog's actions will be looked upon by fellow Guns with a mixture of amusement and annoyance: but mostly annoyance.

Almost any 'proper' whistle that you can think of was developed by the company started many years ago by Joseph Hudson – a Derbyshire farm worker who moved to Birmingham as a result of the Industrial Revolution. The Acme Thunderer and the Silent Dog Whistle are all products of Joseph's factory and are of obvious use to the shooting person, whether to indicate the end of a drive or to keep control of one's dog. Whistles are clearly essential in training a dog for use on the shooting field. Quality and resonance is of utmost importance, as the sound emitted needs to remain constant.

◆

**OPPOSITE**
TRADITIONAL ATTIRE IS SMART, COMFORTABLE AND BLENDS IN WITH THE SURROUNDINGS
**ABOVE**
RETRIEVING BIRDS FROM WATER WOULD BE IMPOSSIBLE WITHOUT
A WELL-TRAINED, BIDDABLE DOG

# The Mid-Morning Break

Depending on how many drives are planned, the mid-morning break is normally taken after the first two, or just before the penultimate drive of the morning. On Bransdale Moor, guests may be offered tea, coffee or Bullshot, together with hot sausages and mustard. James Chapel, director of William Powell Sporting, who is responsible for letting and running all the shoot days, adds, 'we also offer sloe gin or sherry, soft drinks and water as well as chocolate'. In fact many shoots provide a basket of cooked sausages wrapped in tin foil, packets of savoury cheese biscuits, a bottle of champagne, a flask of Bullshot, sloe gin, some beers and mineral water which are brought out to wherever there is a suitable place to stop. Others have a barn to which everyone returns, or, as in the case of the Trippetts shoot on the Hampshire/ Sussex borders, a rather attractive roofed farmyard midden serves very well

**OPPOSITE**
THE CONVERSATION AND CRAIC ARE AN IMPORTANT AND
ENJOYABLE PART OF ANY DAY'S SHOOTING

indeed! Should there be a return back to 'base' then it ought not to be the lunch lodge if this means that boots and outer clothing have to be removed. Certainly a little shelter is welcome but not if it means disrobing and wasting much valuable time.

If the nibbles are hot, then it is probably best to prearrange a probable time of arrival which can then be confirmed via a quick mobile phone call between the host or shoot captain and whoever is responsible for preparing the food. Any delay during the first part of the morning, either because of an unexpectedly big drive or the fact that the Guns are taking a long time picking up with their dogs (and why should they not?) might mean that an intended 10.45 break actually takes place at 11.15, and, while the food will probably not spoil, it is surely better to let someone know rather than it be left to go cold.

How long the break should last is a moot point. Guns who know each other well are, it must be admitted, prone to getting so engrossed in their conversation that it is difficult to get them moving again. On the other hand, such times are an important and enjoyable part of their day and there is often much to discuss: it might be where they've been shooting recently, the current whereabouts of mutual friends or maybe even business. However the length of the break is very important to the keeper and his beating team as well, as it provides them with a chance to do some blanking-in without having the worry of keeping the Guns waiting for too long. There are also situations where birds need to be quietly pushed over the gun ride before being driven back and it is obvious folly to have the Guns anywhere near whilst this is being done. Generally though, half an hour should be sufficient.

ABOVE SAUSAGES AND BULLSHOT ARE OFTEN KEY INGREDIENTS OF THE
TRADITIONAL MID-MORNING BREAK
OPPOSITE AN ATTRACTIVE, COURTYARD SETTING IS THE VENUE FOR
THE MID-MORNING BREAK ON THE TRIPPETTS ESTATE

Until its sale in 2009, the shoot at Linkenholt, near Andover in Hampshire, was for a long time run by Christopher and Amanda Bunbury. According to an article written in *Country Illustrated* magazine (November 1997) by Katie Mahon, the elevenses break for their Guns might have included a glass of chilled rosé wine on a warm September's day partridge shooting or, in the colder months, hot soup served from a thermos. Katie's article contained the following description:

'He [Christopher] is questioned at length as to the mixture, which in fact varies according to availability of fresh ingredients. Christopher's stockpot is their mainspring… the sight of the master removing a large cast-iron pot from the bottom of the aged Aga, lifting off the lid and inhaling with undisguised joy the aromas which escape, is a familiar one. A secret of the flavour is dried wild mushrooms added to game carcasses, slowly producing the bouillon so necessary for good soup.

'Some days the soup may be based on oxtail… a labour of love since it takes at least forty-eight hours to prepare first of all the stew and then to transform the remains into a soup. The oxtail bones, as with all game carcasses, are first oven-baked

HIGH GROUND AND GAME CROPS ON THE LINKENHOLT ESTATE

together with unpeeled shallots, and with a drizzling of olive oil to produce an even more concentrated colour. They are then transferred to a large saucepan with the remains of the oxtail stew, plus a little stock or water, and returned to the Aga for twelve hours. [After the bones have been removed, the resultant soup is whizzed] until smooth in a blender, adding a little more liquid, depending on how thick it is. On really cold days, soups may be given extra bite by the addition of curry or chilli powder. Christopher never adds alcohol to his soups as they cook, knowing that some Guns prefer not to drink while shooting.'

## Tom and Mary's Tomato and Rosemary Soup

Tom Chambers was, in the early 1970s, the part-time keeper for a little shoot in East Yorkshire. His wife Mary cooked the meals. I went once as attendant to one of the Guns and, for various reasons, the morning did not go too well. When we went in for lunch, the total bag stood at one pheasant and five partridges; all but two of which my new dog Jasper had the good fortune to retrieve. Jasper was, in fact, my first ever gundog, an English Springer possessing such individual characteristics that my head keeper said they should qualify him as an act in Bostock and Wombwell's circus. (Apparently Bostock and Wombwell were an early twentieth century travelling enterprise known particularly in the north east of England.). Despite its scarcity of game, the morning was much enjoyed and lunch even more so, especially the soup. As a hungry sixteen-year-old I was keen to report the recipe back to my mother. Almost literally scribbled on the back of a fag-packet, I have kept it ever since. Unfortunately, Jasper, left on trust with the morning's bag and without the opportunity to enjoy the soup, decided to make alternative lunch arrangements and devoured most of the birds!

This soup is also good from the point of view that, once made, it is easily transferable into a flask and pours without mishap.

For 12 people, use the following quantities.

---

55g/2oz unsalted butter
2 medium-sized onions, peeled and sliced
1.2ltr/2pts hot chicken stock
1.5kg/3½lb very ripe red tomatoes (possibly from summer stock frozen individually in the freezer), skinned and roughly chopped
6 tablespoons of water
2 sprigs fresh rosemary
sea salt and fresh ground black pepper

---

Melt the butter in a large saucepan over a moderate heat and cook the onion until it is transparent (about five minutes). Add the stock and cook again for a further ten minutes or so. Liquidise, sieve or pulverise. Meanwhile, in a second pan, place the tomatoes and water, bring to the boil and simmer gently for about quarter of an hour or so. Push through a sieve and then stir the tomato puree into the onion stock. Simmer with the sprigs of rosemary for a further ten minutes; remove the rosemary, season with the salt and pepper and pour into a suitable flask.

## Country Carrot Spicy Soup

Carrot soup was apparently enjoyed as far back as the 1600s. The hint of added curry in this recipe gives it that extra little something often needed on a cold morning. The quantities listed here will serve a team of between six and eight Guns.

---

55g/2oz butter
450g/1lb onions, peeled and sliced
1 tablespoon plain flour
700g/1½lbs carrots, scraped and thinly sliced
1.8ltrs/3½pts chicken stock
salt and pepper
2 teaspoons mild curry powder
2 tablespoons water

---

In a large heavy-bottomed pan or flameproof casserole, gently melt the butter. Dust the onion slices with the flour and add them to the pan; let them sweat rather than brown, for about ten minutes, or until they are soft and slightly golden. Add the carrots and the chicken stock. Season and bring to the boil before simmering (uncovered) for about half an hour, or until the carrots are soft. Push the soup through a sieve or whiz it in a blender before returning it to the pan in which it was cooked. Mix the curry powder with the water until it makes a smooth paste. Stir this into the soup and simmer gently for a further fifteen minutes before decanting into a couple of thermos flasks or jugs.

## Frank Boddy's Bullshot

Frank Boddy, shoot captain for the Ripley Castle, Nidd, Hob Green, Cayton, Eagle Hall, Ashfold Side estates and also the Hardcastle and Heathfield moors, serves this unusual variation on the usual Bullshot recipe. Frank claims that for best results it should be mixed up the evening before the shooting day and left to marinate overnight. The quantities given are more than sufficient for nine Guns, making approximately three litres in total.

2 x 400g tins Heinz oxtail soup

4 x 415g tins Baxters beef consommé

200ml bottle Schweppes tomato juice cocktail (or V8 is even better)

4 tablespoons Geo. Watkins mushroom ketchup

a few drops of Lea & Perrins Worcestershire sauce

a few less drops of McIlhenny Co. Tabasco pepper sauce

a pinch of paprika or cayenne pepper (or both if it is a very cold day!)

*To serve*

Knorr beef bouillon paste

Marmite

sherry

FRANK BODDY OF THE RIPLEY CASTLE SHOOT DISPENSING THE RESULTS OF HIS OWN PARTICULAR
RECIPE FOR BULLSHOT (COURTESY OF TIM HARDY AND FRANK BODDY)

Mix all the ingredients together in a large bowl. Cover and leave overnight. The next day, bring to the boil in a large saucepan and stir in one heaped tablespoon of Knorr beef bouillon paste and one twisted table fork of Marmite. Stir well and bring to a simmer before adding (preferably) Croft Original sherry to taste ('do not spoil it with vodka or similar!' says Frank). Store in a thermos until required.

## Alternative Drinks

As well as soups and Bullshot, fruit liqueurs, beer and/or champagne are a traditional mid-morning offering. Why not combine the latter two by making up a jug of Black Velvet? The usual combination is half Guinness to half champagne. If you are creating Black Velvet in individual glasses, choose whether to pour the two ingredients gently together or, as the aficionados claim it must be done, trickle the champagne over the back of a spoon and allow it to run onto the Guinness. By this technique, the layers should remain separate. Always have a few cans of non-alcoholic drinks or small bottles of mineral water on offer as well, especially on a warm September day: also, not everyone wants to drink alcohol even in moderation when shooting. William Asprey remarks that '… the mid-morning drink can work if you are not shooting so well, but if I'm shooting well I tend to forego it as I don't want to upset my shooting!'

## Hip Flasks

Hip flasks make a good present for anyone involved in outdoor pursuits. Antique ones of good quality and which still have a serviceable leak-proof cork stopper are also very collectable but unfortunately can be quite expensive. They are always well worth looking out for at car boot sales and auctions of sporting memorabilia. Personally, I have always had a fancy to find one which originates from America in the days of prohibition, especially if it happened to have been one owned by a lady as, so it is said, they were quite regularly kept hidden on the thigh by means of a garter. Now there would be a real conversation piece as one offered it round the assembled shooting party…

To clean a metal flask, most people agree that the best method is to take a teaspoon of bicarbonate of soda mixed with hot water and carefully pour the mixture into the neck via a small funnel, a piping bag, or the top section of an inverted washing-up bottle. Leave it overnight and rinse well with cold water in the morning. To store a flask during the summer, make sure that the inside is completely dry and pour in a teaspoon of sugar; this will prevent any stale odours that might otherwise taint future contents. Of course, if you can find an excuse to use your hip flask on a regular basis, the problems of cleaning or eradicating stale smells will never arise due to the fact that it is permanently sterilised by your favourite tipple.

## *Liqueurs and other hip flask fillers*

You will no doubt be pleased to learn that, according to M. I. Fisher, writing in *Liqueurs: A Dictionary and Survey*, '… good liqueurs have always been both digestive and curative'. Should you be offered a vermouth as your pre-prandial drink, then it may be as well to realise that, again according to Fisher, the word 'vermouth' is the literal translation of the English 'wormwood', derived directly from the Anglo-Saxon *wermod*, meaning 'mind preserver'. Of interest also is that the word 'liqueur' is derived from the Latin *liquefacere*, apparently meaning 'to melt, to make liquid, to dissolve'. You might like to mention either of these connections should there ever be a lull in the conversation!

## *Whisky*

Whisky, especially when mixed with Drambuie to create a Rusty Nail, is the obvious hip flask filler, as is a Percy Special, which is equal parts of whisky and cherry brandy. However, should you wish just to top up with a single malt, Loch Fyne Whiskies, based at Inveraray, Argyll, advise that 'those from the lowlands are the most gentle; mild, almost wine-like [while] Islay whiskies are unguided missiles in the wrong hands – you will either love them or wonder what the attraction is in smelling hospitals'.

'STEADY … IT'S TOO GOOD TO WASTE!'

It would be sacrilege to suggest that one should ever add lemonade or ginger to a single malt (and, by the way, according to Loch Fyne Whiskies, 'There is no such thing as a double malt unless you are with your rich father-in-law at the bar [when it would then be] termed a "large one"'. Incidentally, should you ever be tempted to add a mixer to any sort of spirit in a hip flask, make sure that the flask is made of glass. Anything else is quite likely to split apart at the soldering due to the build-up of gases.

### The King's Ginger

The King's Ginger is a liqueur that was specifically formulated in 1903 by Berry Bros for King Edward VII. Rich and zesty, it was created to stimulate and revivify His Majesty and has apparently been 'appreciated by bon viveurs ever since'. It is made by the careful maceration of ginger root enlivened by the judicious addition of a citrus flavour in the form of lemon peel. Berry Bros & Rudd also describe it thus: 'Although warming and heartening on a cold day as originally intended, it is a splendidly uplifting tonic to be enjoyed on its own all year round as well as in any number of cocktails and long drinks.' Vicky Williams, their PR manager, suggests that it is perfect in a hip flask (although care must be taken when imbibing on a shooting day as it is 41 percent by volume), especially if used to create a Rusty Tack. Simply mix together equal quantities of The King's Ginger and Cutty Sark Scotch whisky: sounds marvellous!

### Sloe Gin

There's sloe gin, and then there's sloe gin… Make it how you like (and there is a recipe below for one 'classic' method) but if you want to buy a bottle ready-made it's obviously a matter of personal choice and taste. Gordon's make a very good one, as does Nick Radclyffe at Foxdenton Estate. The estate was first acquired by the family in 1367 and has remained in their ownership ever since. In 2001, Nick took over the running of the estate and has, in the intervening years, developed a company which runs parallel to the family's hunting and shooting history. It has made available to the public fruit liqueurs which were first made for personal enjoyment by the family. The strength of their sloe gin is, at 29 percent, stronger than nearly all the others on the market, a factor which, according to Nick, 'gives it a real bite'. It is, he says, 'a recognisably different sloe gin'.

### Lovage and Brandy

Lovage liqueur is famously made by Phillips of Bristol and was originally distilled from herbs grown in the county, and to a secret recipe handed down through generations of the family. Unusually for a liqueur, it is only 5.3 percent alcohol by volume but is usually added two parts lovage to one of brandy as a hip flask filler so that immediately changes the situation!

## RECIPES FOR HOME-MADE LIQUEURS

Devising your own liqueurs is a lovely idea and collecting the necessary fruit ingredients is the perfect way to spend a mild autumn afternoon. All that is then required is to add a certain amount of sugar and top up with your choice of spirits. In practice, however, unless one sticks rigidly to a known recipe it is better to restrict oneself to filling a hip flask with a commercially produced liqueur where one has at least some idea as to the alcoholic content. Drink your own concoction at home by the fireside by all means, but be wary of bringing it out on a shooting day – a chief constable of our acquaintance sensibly maintains that 'the possession of a firearm, even if unloaded, bears responsibilities and I most certainly wouldn't recommend anyone being remotely drunk around guns'.

### *Classic Sloe Gin*

Pick the sloes in the autumn, but don't worry about the traditionalists who insist that the fruit should not be picked until it has had a frost on it – it makes no difference at all to the end product. Again, according to traditionalists, each sloe must be pricked with a fork, but that is very time consuming and tedious, and I find that it is easiest to bruise them and split the skin by using the end of a wooden rolling pin. Alternatively, freeze them as a single layer on a tray for a few days, after which time the skins will have burst.

---

450g/1lb sloes
225g/8oz castor or brown sugar
1 x 70cl bottle gin

---

Nick Radclyffe's paternal grandfather wrote of shooting with Sir John Kelk at Tedworth House, Hampshire, at the end of the Victorian period and recalled that Kelk was very particular about his cellar, even going so far as to fill his guests' flasks personally in the morning before shooting:
'One morning, on nearing the rendezvous, our host turned to us and said: "By Jove, you fellows, I am most awfully sorry I forgot to fill your flasks this morning." Now personally I never carried a flask out shooting, and such was the case with five out of the seven guns present. Naturally this statement caused a sensation, since five or six flasks had been given to the butler each morning, and had been regularly filled by Kelk himself with his best liqueurs. It did not make matters any better when he was assured that doubtless our valets had greatly appreciated this pretty bit of attention on his part.'

◆

Place the washed and prepared sloes into a wide-necked, screw-top glass container (a large Kilner jar is good), add the sugar and the gin and close the lid firmly. Shake daily for a few days, every other day for a few more and then once a week for a couple of months. Leave for as long as you can (sloe gin made in early October is technically ready to drink by Christmas, but the longer you leave it, the better tasting it will be). When ready strain through muslin or even a paper coffee filter and bottle.

## Blackberry Whisky

Make blackberry whisky (or brandy) by using the same methods and quantities as for the recipe for *Classic Sloe Gin* above. It is, however, obviously not necessary to prick or bruise the fruit, though it should be rinsed well under cold running water.

## 'Slivovitz' – Russian Plum Brandy

As vodka rather than brandy is the main alcoholic ingredient in this liqueur, maybe it should technically be 'Plum Vodka'? It is, however, based on a Balkan recipe from days gone by.

1kg/2¼lbs ripe plums
225g/8oz sugar
1 ltr/1¾pts vodka
250ml/8fl oz brandy

Slice the plums in half and remove the stones before putting the fruit into a very large Kilner jar or similar. Add the sugar, vodka and brandy. Seal and then shake the contents on a daily basis until the sugar has more or less dissolved. Shake weekly after that and finally, after three or four months, strain, bottle and leave the liquid for about nine months to mature. Use the plums in a tart or dessert – or just eat as they are, with ice-cream!

Christopher West, manager of the Hebridean Smokehouse, has a slightly different take on the subject of fruit-infused vodka drinks. His method is, apparently, to empty out a third of the bottle and pour in handfuls of blueberries, the skins of which have been slightly scored with the aid of a cheese grater. The bottle is then shaken hard and left for an hour or two before drinking.

Taken from a letter of thanks from a guest to his shooting host in 1959:

'... not only did I enjoy the day's shooting overall, but I think it is fair to say that the little snifter we had with the sausage rolls did much to make the drive before lunch my personal best. Birds came fast and furious and, were it not for the further calming effects of my loader's hip flask which he so generously shared, I think I might have got into quite a flap. As it was, and with him "spotting" for me, I had the most wonderful time and was ready to tell one and all about it when we went in to join the ladies! On reflection, I might well have bored them... if so, my most utmost apologies...'

# Guns! This Way for Lunch

The general advice to anyone contemplating a career in shooting and planning to buy a pair of breeches is well known: perceived wisdom has it that you should choose a pair in as large a size as possible, so that you can grow into them as a result of the substantial lunch portions you will undoubtedly enjoy over the years!

In a shooting magazine some years ago, an article suggested that modern sportsmen and women should be offered a more healthy option at the lunch table and that Shepherd's Pie and swede should make way for salmon and salads. In fact the writer was not offering any new or radical thinking as even in the early 1900s, lunch might have consisted of any variation of hot or cold food, depending upon where it was served. Edward VII had it that two hot dishes should always be sent down from the kitchens at Sandringham, together with a selection of lobster or chicken salads.

**OPPOSITE TOP** LUNCH AT HOLFIELD GRANGE, ESSEX
**BELOW LEFT** GAME TERRINE CAN BE A GOOD WAY OF USING UP THOSE ODD PIECES OF MEAT FREQUENTLY LEFT AT THE BOTTOM OF THE FREEZER AT THE END OF EACH SEASON (COURTESY OF PHILIP WATTS)
**BELOW RIGHT** TO SAVE VALUABLE MINUTES ON A DARK WINTER'S DAY, MANY SHOOTS EITHER SERVE THE CHEESE BOARD AT THE SAME TIME AS PUDDING, OR DISPENSE WITH THE LATTER ALTOGETHER

Royal lunches served at Broadlands during the 1960s and 1970s, though, were a different matter and typically consisted of a light stew made of thinly sliced lamb cutlets, pearl barley and onions, served with potatoes, or a beef hotpot. The pudding course was normally a steamed pudding with, perhaps, syrup, stewed apple or chocolate. Then head gamekeeper Harry Grass and his family apparently considered these meals to be insubstantial for a cold winter's shoot day and, according to writer, archivist and historian David S.D. Jones, 'would not have eaten any of the food, even if it were to have been offered – although they were happy to accept a glass of cherry brandy from the butler'!

At Bransdale Moor, north of Helmsley, in North Yorkshire, the shoot is run on a commercial basis by William Powell Sporting: lunch generally starts with soup and a collection of cold meats, pies, salads, and smoked salmon before cheese, fruit cake and coffee. As a Yorkshireman myself, I know that the cheese and fruitcake combination works well – as indeed does cold apple pie and cheese, preferably Wensleydale. Interestingly, the Bransdale shoot has a mobile lunch hut which can be tractor-pulled to whatever beat is being driven. Although unusual in this day and age, this custom follows on from the trend of Edwardian times, when a horse-drawn luncheon van would magically appear at a designated point at a required time.

Whilst there might be some merit in serving a cold seafood platter and salad on the moors during August, it would not, I fear, find many enthusiastic followers after a morning spent in the bracing elements of a wintry December day. Indeed, James Benson at Benson's of Broadway tells me that they always provide a hearty lunch which never fails to warm everyone up before they step outside again for the afternoon's sport.

James's company is one of several outside catering groups who specialise in providing lunches for shooting parties. Unless you happen to be fortunate enough to have household staff, it is probably the most practical option available to any host – irrespective of whether the intention is to provide a sit-down meal indoors or soup, baked potatoes and chilli-con-carne in a far-flung barn. Outside caterers tend to be imaginative in their menus too and even if the traditional Shepherd's Pie is on offer, the usual plain creamed potato mash is often enlivened by the addition of kale, leeks and a little grain mustard as well as cream and butter. Fortunately, there appears to be no shortage of freelance shoot-lunch providers – many of whom can be found on the internet – all of whom offer a bewildering array of mouth-watering choices.

OPPOSITE TOP AT BRANSDALE, GUNS ARE SERVED LUNCH IN THIS SUPERBLY CONSTRUCTED TRAILER WHICH CAN BE TOWED TO WHEREVER IT IS REQUIRED (COURTESY OF JAMES CHAPEL, WILLIAM POWELL SPORTING)
OPPOSITE BELOW A HORSE-DRAWN LUNCHEON TRAILER IN USE A CENTURY EARLIER THAN THE ONE AT BRANSDALE (COURTESY OF D. S. D. JONES)

SHEPHERD'S PIE IS A STAPLE OF MANY A SHOOT LUNCH

For example:

'Shepherd's pie with leek, potato and cheese topping; lamb and vegetable hot pot; chicken and mushroom pie; chicken and cider casserole; spiced baked chicken breasts with mango chutney and pilau rice; steak, kidney and mushroom pie; beef and Guinness casserole with dumplings; braised beef in red wine with shallots and mushrooms; beef lasagne with garlic bread; boiled gammon served with Cumberland sauce and bubble and squeak; pork and leek sausages with mashed potato and onion gravy; venison sausages with red onion marmalade served with mustard mash; game pie with redcurrant jelly; mixed fish au gratin.'

These delicious main courses can then be followed by delectable puddings, such as:

'Glazed lemon tart; treacle tart; sticky toffee pudding with toffee sauce; tarte tatin with whipped cream; pear and blackberry crumble; sticky plum tart; apricot tart; apple and frangipani slice with warm caramel sauce; syrup sponge pudding with lemon and syrup sauce; chocolate sponge pudding with dark chocolate sauce; chocolate roulade; chocolate and pear tart; bread and butter pudding.'

APRICOT TART FEATURES ON THE MENU OF MANY OUTSIDE CATERERS

Most companies then offer a cheese board with biscuits and fresh fruit, tea and coffee and, once the shooting day has finished, tea with scones and cream, cakes and biscuits.

It might just be added that being involved in outside catering is not without its complications. Cara Richardson, based at Aviemore, Inverness-shire, tells of an occasion when she'd been booked to cook for a group of five German stalkers at a lodge at Kilchoan on Ardnamurchan. They were due to arrive at five pm but to begin with she wasn't unduly worried by their absence. As time went on, and they still did not appear, not only was supper spoiling, she was naturally becoming extremely worried about them. Eventually, at ten pm the missing stalkers were discovered hungry but happy, having let themselves in to totally the wrong lodge, some two miles down the road!

## Pre-Prandial Delights

Most shoots will not, in the interests of practicality and the need to get back out quickly, include a starter course at lunchtime. However a few 'nibbles' can always be offered alongside the pre-lunch drinks. During the days when the Linkenholt shoot was being run by Christopher and Amanda Bunbury, their guest Guns were often treated to various accompaniments including quail's eggs on garlic croutons and crostini, or even tiny white bread sandwiches filled with air-dried ham, soaked in beaten egg and then deep-fried.

On a shoot recently I was offered what looked like a simple round of toast on top of which a slice of goat's cheese had been lightly grilled – 'nothing much exciting in this' was my first thought – until I bit into it and discovered a glorious and very unexpected sweetness, produced by the drizzling of a little honey on the toast. You might think this an unusual and perhaps even unpleasant combination but it worked really well. The host was Danish and, as a nation, the Danes seem to create a great many unexpectedly sweet/savoury dishes.

Pâtés of all descriptions can suit the start of a shooting lunch – as they do on many other occasions. In the early days of Victoria's reign, the Reverend Sidney Smith (1771–1845), was quoted as saying, 'My idea of heaven is eating pâté de fois gras to the sound of trumpets.' Needless to say, this frivolous attitude and keenness for the good things in life did not sit well with the reverend's somewhat dour contemporaries, more than one of whom opined that Smith 'would never make a bishop'!

## *Chicken and Rabbit Liver Pâté*
A recipe from Christopher and Amanda Bunbury: it is best served with Melba toast.

LINKENHOLT – A 'MECCA' FOR SPORTING GOURMANDS IN THE DAYS OF
CHRIS AND ANGELA BUNBURY!

225g/8oz chicken livers

225g/8oz rabbit livers

2 shallots, peeled and chopped

1 clove garlic, crushed

225g/8oz chanterelle mushrooms

1 small glass brandy

zest of half an orange

seasoning

Sauté the shallots in butter in a large frying pan until very tender, adding the garlic halfway through. Stir in the mushrooms and cook through. When ready, push to one side of the pan and add the livers. Briefly fry these on both sides, taking care not to overcook, and then mix with the shallots. Pour a small glass of brandy into the pan, ignite, allow the alcohol to burn off, then take the pan off the heat. Blend all the ingredients together in a processor, with seasoning to taste, and add the zest of the orange before placing in small ramekins. Chill before serving.

## Game Terrine

Despite what some people might say about game being served as part of a shooting lunch (see below), it would be a shame not to utilise all those odd pieces frequently left at the bottom of the freezer. The quantities given here will make terrine enough for a team of eight Guns.

1kg/2¼lb game meat – pheasant, partridge, rabbit, hare, pigeon or duck – off the bone

12 rashers of streaky bacon

450g/1lb sausage meat

225g/8oz chopped liver

freshly made breadcrumbs taken from two thick slices of bread

2 cloves garlic, chopped

1 egg

1 handful of flat-leaf or curly parsley and thyme, chopped and mixed together

1 'glug' red wine

1 'glug' brandy (optional)

1 small handful pistachio nuts, crushed

1 handful gherkins, chopped

2 diced and cooked carrots

sea salt and black pepper

a little olive oil (for frying the meat)

DESPITE THE OPINION OF SOME,
THERE CAN BE LITTLE POINT
IN SHOOTING GAME OF ANY SORT
IF IT IS NOT TO BE ENJOYED
AT THE LUNCH TABLE

## *Swinton Estate Grouse*

Were it not for a quirk of history, Edwardian estate owners might well have been emulating Swinton Park rather than Sandringham, for legend has it that this north Yorkshire estate was almost purchased by the Royal Family – until that is, they are said to have seen the height of the pheasants, which they maintained were too high! Be that fact or fiction, it is an undoubted truth that Swinton remains a prime sporting estate which extends to some twenty thousand or more acres. Nowadays, the grouse moors take up about nine thousand acres and the pheasant shoot about five thousand, with the remainder of the land being either tenanted or given over to forestry.

Owned by Mark and Felicity Cunliffe-Lister (Lord and Lady Masham) Swinton Park is well-known, not only for its game shooting opportunities, but also as the perfect country hotel and retreat where it is possible to indulge in all manner of entertainments ranging from off-road adventures to clay pigeon shooting and relaxing in the hotel spa. There is an excellent cookery school which has a vast array of courses and demonstrations on offer. Grouse-shooters take their lunch at one of the moorland huts while pheasant Guns eat in the hotel's private dining-room where high ceilings, gold-covered plaster mouldings and a large marble fireplace make it an eating experience as memorable as any of the pheasant drives. In addition, there is also the opportunity for the low-ground Guns to dine in the Deer Hut, which is also sometimes used to cater for clay pigeon shooting guests. Swinton's guests sometimes have the opportunity to taste the estate's grouse, prepared to the following recipe (which serves four).

WERE IT NOT FOR A QUIRK OF FATE, SWINTON PARK COULD WELL HAVE BECOME A
ROYAL RESIDENCE (COURTESY OF FELICITY CUNLIFFE-LISTER, SWINTON PARK)

4 young oven-ready grouse
4 slices of pancetta or streaky bacon
4 sprigs rosemary
4 sprigs of thyme
12 juniper berries
4 cloves garlic, peeled and crushed
100g/3½oz butter
Maldon salt and freshly ground pepper

Season the grouse with salt and pepper. Place pieces of rosemary, thyme and a garlic clove in the cavity of each bird and truss it. Place a slice of pancetta or bacon over the breast of the grouse and secure it with string. Melt the butter in a large ovenproof frying pan over a moderately high heat. When the butter is hot, seal the grouse on all sides. Place the birds in a roasting tin in an oven heated to gas mark 7/220°C and cook for 20 to 30 minutes (depending on size), basting them regularly. When cooked, remove from the oven, cover with foil and allow to rest for five minutes before serving on croutons, if liked, accompanied by game chips and a game sauce.

*To make croutons*
4 slices of thick white bread, cut into rounds large enough to make a base for each bird
200g/7oz game pâté
55g/2oz butter

In the frying pan used for sealing the grouse, add a little more butter and, over a moderate heat, fry the slices of bread for about a minute on each side until golden and crisp. Spread a little of the pâté over each slice. Keep warm until ready to serve.

*To make game chips*
600g/1lb 3oz potatoes
oil for deep frying
Maldon salt

Peel the potatoes and slice them wafer thin with a mandolin, or by hand with a sharp knife. Place them in a bowl of water for 20 minutes (this is to remove the starch). Heat the oil in a deep fryer or wok to 190°C. Dry the potato slices thoroughly and then fry them in the oil in batches for a couple of minutes each until they are crisp and golden. Drain the chips on paper towels and sprinkle a little salt over them. Keep warm until ready to serve.

*To make game sauce*
500ml/18fl oz game stock
100ml/3½fl oz port
1 tablespoon redcurrant jelly

Place the stock and port in a saucepan and bring to a strong simmer: boil uncovered until reduced to a sticky sauce. Stir in the redcurrant jelly and keep warm until ready to serve.

*To serve the grouse*

Place a crouton on each plate. Remove the string from the grouse and place them on the croutons. Drizzle the sauce around the birds and place the chips alongside together with a handful of watercress.

## Two Bird Bake

The *Two Bird Bake* is another of Jill Knowles's recipes (see also *Venison with Brie and Blackcurrant*) which has proved popular with many shooting people as a result of being included in recipe leaflets published in connection with the various BASC 'Game's On' promotions up and down the country. It will serve a small family team of six Guns.

6 partridge breasts and 6 pheasant breasts
1 large onion, chopped
4 rashers of streaky bacon or pancetta, cubed
75g/2¾oz of butter
75g/2¾oz of mushrooms, chopped
1 dessertspoon juniper berries, crushed
1 dessertspoon coriander seeds, crushed
a head of sage leaves
salt and pepper
150ml/5fl oz double cream
150ml/5fl oz Marsala wine
600ml/1pt game stock (made from bird carcasses)
1 tablespoon of cornflour

*For the breadcrumbs*
5–6 slices of sliced bread made into breadcrumbs
55g/2oz butter
equal amount of vegetable oil

Melt the butter in a large frying pan and add the oil. Add the breadcrumbs to the pan and turn frequently to allow steam to escape. Keep frying until breadcrumbs are brown.

Next fry off the onions and bacon in the butter until soft. Add the mushrooms and stir with crushed juniper berries and coriander. In a separate pan, fry off pheasant and partridge breasts until just sealed.

Add stock, cream and Marsala to the onion, bacon and mushroom mix and bring to the boil. Thicken the sauce with slaked cornflour (mix the cornflour with a little water until creamy) before pouring the sauce over the pheasant and partridge breasts and topping with fried breadcrumbs. Oven bake for 15 minutes at gas mark 6/180°C.

## NON-GAME SUGGESTIONS

Recipe books are full of ideas for warming and sustaining main courses and it is simply a question of selecting something suitable for your particular group. As a general rule, slow cooking methods not only work best with the cheaper cuts but can also be left to their own devices once prepared, allowing everyone concerned to get on with far more interesting things – like shooting!

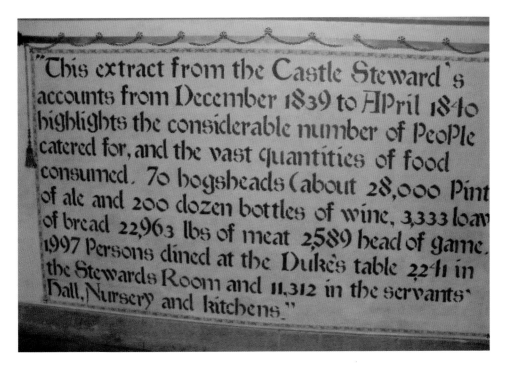

**ABOVE** INTERESTING TEXT TO BE FOUND ON THE WALL AT BELVOIR CASTLE, LEICESTERSHIRE
(COURTESY OF KATE BOWLES, BELVOIR CASTLE & ESTATES)
**OVERLEAF** THE DEER HUT AT SWINTON IS USED AS A LUNCH VENUE BY BOTH PHEASANT GUNS
AND CLAY SHOOTING GUESTS (COURTESY OF FELICITY CUNLIFFE-LISTER, SWINTON PARK)

The shoot dining-room at Belvoir Castle in Leicestershire is, like that at Eastnor (see page 94), quite sumptuous and diners cannot fail to be impressed by the warmth of their surroundings. On a good many of their days the Guns are offered a substantial 'twelveses', which is taken out on the shoot, with guests then returning to the Castle at the end of the day for a late lunch. Typical menus include steak and ale pie, coq au vin, roast lamb, roast beef, roast loin of pork or gammon with Cumberland sauce, all of which are served with potatoes and seasonal vegetables. On other occasions, it may be that lunch is taken at midday in the shoot room and then, after a couple more drives, Guns come back in for afternoon tea. Belvoir Castle is obviously well used to entertaining – as the photograph on page 85 testifies.

At Loyton Lodge in Devon, shoot lunches are held in an annexe to the main building. A huge and very beautiful rustic table fills the centre of the room, whilst recipes from chef Nick Pyle fulfil the discerning requirements of the guests! Experience has taught both Nick and owner Alick Barnes that, for lunch, relatively simple food goes down well. A typical menu might, for example, be 'meat and two veg' followed by a pile of doughnuts and, bringing up the rear, a whole Stilton cheese. (The reason for the success of the doughnuts is apparently two-fold: often forbidden food to males of a certain age with expanding waistlines, out of sight of their wives, these treats can be surreptitiously enjoyed; secondly, they can easily be wrapped in a napkin and taken out to the drives after lunch!)

## Braised Ox Cheeks with Red Wine and Onions

Nick Pyle enjoys introducing some of the more unusual cuts of meat to his menus – hence this delicious main course dish, which will feed 12–14 people.

4–6 ox cheeks trimmed (ask your butcher to trim these for you)
vegetable oil
4 large onions, diced
2 carrots, peeled and diced
2 sticks celery, diced
2 bay leaves
a small bunch of thyme
5 cloves garlic, peeled and crushed
1 bottle good red wine
1.5ltr/3pts beef stock
salt and pepper

Season the cheeks and seal them for two to three minutes on each side in a hot pan with a little oil, then set aside. Fry off the vegetables and herbs in a large pan with a little oil until soft and golden. Add the red wine, bring to the boil and simmer to reduce by half. Then add the stock and the cheeks. Cover and cook in the oven for four to five hours at gas mark 2/150°C. (When done, the cheeks should be soft.) Remove the cheeks from the sauce and set aside to rest for 10 minutes. Reduce the sauce until thick, slice the cheeks and arrange on a warmed serving dish. Ladle over the sauce. Serve with creamy mash and buttered kale, cabbage or purple sprouting.

## Bowden 'Fox Curry'

It isn't just the grand shoots that have culinary traditions. The Bowden shoot – a modest DIY affair that puts down a couple of hundred birds each season – lies in what used to be countryside but is now hedged in by executive villas on one side and a motorway on the other. Nevertheless, in its steep valley with pheasants bursting from the bracken and woodcock skimming through the coverts it is a very traditional English shoot. And it has its own traditions: in particular 'fox curry'.

There is little doubt that encroaching suburbia has increased the fox population

GUNS ENJOY CONVERSATION IN THE SHOOTING TRAILER AT BRANSDALE, NORTH YORKSHIRE
(COURTESY OF JAMES CHAPEL, WILLIAM POWELL SPORTING)

AT EASTNOR, GUNS CAN ENJOY THE GRANDEUR OF THE DINING-ROOM'S SURROUNDINGS AS THEY
EAT LUNCH... (COURTESY OF SIMON FOSTER AND THE HERVEY-BATHURST FAMILY)

Cream the butter and sugar until light and fluffy, then add the breadcrumbs, well-beaten eggs, jam and the bicarbonate of soda (the latter having been dissolved in a dessertspoon of tepid water). Mix well and put into a buttered pudding basin, leaving room for the mixture to swell and rise. Cover with buttered paper or foil, tied round the bowl with a piece of string, and steam in a double boiler, large pan or bain-marie for two hours. Turn out on a heated serving dish and serve hot (with a dash of rum drizzled over if you like) accompanied by custard or fresh cream.

## CHEESES

In recent years there has been an enormous interest in cheese-making – old recipes have been revived and new ones developed using traditional methods, and milk from rare breeds of animals. Local cheeses always add a little something to the conventional cheese board. James Benson, who caters for many Gloucestershire shoots, often suggests including Oxford Blue, Oxford Isis (which he claims is as close to a British version of Calvados Camembert as he has found) and the delightful sounding Birdwood Blue Heaven. The West Country has a wide variety of cheeses, the best-known of which must be Cheddar in all its different guises. Blue Vinney is a hard, white, blue-veined cheese originating from Dorset. Also available are Cornish Yarg (the name sounds Cornish, but is, in fact, the maker's name, Gray, spelt

backwards!), Curworthy and Devon Garland. Tymsboro, produced on a farm near Bath, is a goat's cheese described as having the taste of 'lemon sorbet and apples'. If you're searching for something really different, there is the Beenleigh Blue, which is made from the milk of sheep grazed on Dartmoor. Like many speciality cheeses, it is seasonal but fortunately comes into its own just in time for the shooting season. For a Brie-style cheese, look out for Sharpham Full Fat Soft Cheese produced from a herd of Jersey cows that feeds in the meadows alongside the river Dart.

From Herefordshire comes Finn, hand-made in the village of Dorstone, by Charlie Westhead – apparently it is named after his dog! Also produced in Dorstone is Ragstone – a medium-fat, matured cheese derived from unpasteurised goat's milk. Produced in the same county is Hereford Hop, a hard pasteurised cheese wrapped in hops (the hops are crunchy, with the slightly yeasty taste associated with beer, whilst the cheese is mellow, sweet and buttery). Shropshire Blue has its followers and, moving into Wales, there is Y-Fenni,

IN THE OPINION OF SOME, STILTON CHEESE AND GINGER CAKE MAKE AN IDEAL COMBINATION

produced with the addition of parsley and mustard seeds. In the heart of west Wales can be found Golden Cenarth. Snowdonia cheeses include the rather alarming sounding Green Thunder and Black Bomber varieties. Also to be found in Wales are Llangloffan, Pencarreg Brie, Caws Fferm Teifi (an aged, Gouda-style cheese) and Llanboidy, made from the milk of Red Poll cattle. Caerphilly is, however, probably the best known of all the Welsh cheeses.

As the majority of cow's milk is produced down the western side and middle of Britain, it is not surprising to find so many different varieties of cheese originating from those areas. Well-known types include Cheshire, Red Leicester and, of course, Stilton. Long Clawson Stilton has a delicious creamy texture and is made in a village outside Melton Mowbray.

Robert Gibbons, writing in *The Field* in October 2010, describes a shoot lunch at which he was served 'a large blue Cheshire cheese, celery, pickled walnuts and ginger cake… with a choice of vintage port or an aged calvados.' He continues, 'The custom of having

Stilton accompanied by ginger cake seems to be dying out, which is a pity as they make a great combination'.

Less well-known cheeses are Sage Derby and Coldwick. Another variation on the Derby is Fowler's Little Derby, perversely nowadays made in Warwickshire because the Fowler family moved there from Derbyshire in 1918.

Yorkshire, too, offers a great selection of cheeses: the best-selling Yorkshire Blue, for instance, is a very creamy version of a Stilton type, whilst 'Old Peculiar' Swaledale has the delightful addition of a Theakston's Yorkshire ale. Amongst others are Mrs Bell's Blue; Buffalo Blue, Byland Blue, Old York; Basilano; Smoked Jersey; Coverdale; Cotherstone; Katy's White Lavender and Rydale. Across the Pennines in Lancashire is the crumbly, pale-coloured, buttery and slightly salty-tasting cheese of the same name. Head directly north-east into Northumberland and you will encounter Admiral Collingwood and Baltic, both with rinds washed in local ale. Others include Redesdale ewe's milk cheese. Highland cheese makers specialise in soft cheeses, of which Crowdie (said to have been introduced by the Vikings), is probably the best-known. Others include Caboc, a rich cream cheese rolled in oatmeal, Lanark Blue – made from unpasteurised milk taken from ewes who graze the heather-covered hills of Strathclyde and available only from June to January – Dunlop and Langskaill. Across the water in Ireland there is the classic Irish Cheddar; Cashel Blue, the creamiest of blue cheeses; rich, strong, Camembert-style Cooleeney, made from unpasteurised cow's milk; and Coolea, a nutty, sweet Gouda-style cheese made from pasteurised cow's milk.

## *Buying and storing cheese*

Where possible, buy pieces of hard and semi-hard cheese cut fresh from the whole cheese as ready-cut is likely to go stale more quickly. Do not buy cheese that has cracks running from the edges, or is darker in the middle than it is on the outside: it is already stale and in the process of drying out. Likewise, avoid cheese that is sweating, as it is a sure sign that it has been previously stored at too high a temperature and, as a result, the flavour may well be impaired. However, according to Forman & Field, London-based suppliers of 'fine fresh foods', 'a slight bloom on a cut surface of cheese is a good sign and shows that the atmosphere is nice and humid.' Semi-soft cheeses, such as Brie, which have a chalky layer running through the middle are not ripe and will taste dry and tangy. Do not take this home in the fond hope that it will improve with keeping – the very complicated process of ripening is best left to the producer and is unlikely to be replicated at home.

To get the best from any cheese, it needs to be kept and served carefully. Debbie Bell, who has a stall at Easingwold market in Yorkshire, feels that 'cheese should be wrapped in greaseproof paper and kept in the salad drawer of the fridge before being brought out two hours before you need it. If you have a larder, then that's the best place to keep cheeses like mature Cheddar. Generally, light destroys the B vitamin, so keep it in the dark.' Forman & Field also suggest that the best way of storing cheese is to keep it in the salad drawer of your fridge, or 'in a Tupperware box along with a carrot' as either of these environments create moisture and humidity for the cheese. They too recommend taking cheese from the fridge a minimum of forty-five minutes before it is required, to allow it to come up to room temperature.

## The Five-Minute Bell

In Rosie Nickerson's book *How to be Asked Again*, a superb and very amusing illustration by Oliver Preston shows a line of red wine bottles leading from the front steps of the house towards the back of a shooting vehicle, beside which stands the keeper and a colleague. The keeper is remarking 'It's the only way of getting the Guns out again after lunch.' Perhaps this is so amusing because it rings so true!

Rosie advises not to dawdle once lunch is over and your host has announced that you have only five minutes left. 'Any last minute kit changes or finding more cartridges must be done right away. Wandering about… while everyone else waits for you in their vehicles is just not on. The beaters will have blanked in, the birds will be edgy, and you need to be absolutely ready on time.'

A shoot owner of my acquaintance claims to have solved the problem of tardy Guns by having on the wall above where he sits a huge clock of the kind that one used to find in railway waiting-rooms and schools. The clock is kept ten minutes ahead of real time and the Guns' attention is drawn to it fifteen minutes before they should be on their pegs. The host says that now fewer people have wristwatches because of relying on mobile phones to tell them the time, no one has yet noticed the time discrepancy!

Finally, let me tell you about one particular day on a large shoot in the south of England where the head keeper, eventually driven to distraction by the Guns being continually late after lunch, started the drive at the agreed time of 2.30, even though he knew that there was no one on the pegs. The Guns and their loaders arrived halfway through the drive to find pheasants flying fast and furious over the empty gun line! As one might imagine, heated words were exchanged, but the keeper was so highly thought of that he remained in his job and the Guns were subsequently found to be on their pegs at 2.30 – at least for the remainder of that particular season.

# Lunch on the Go

A break for a sporting lunch out in the open or under the flimsy shelter of a ramshackle barn is no new thing. According to *The Oxford Companion to Food*, 'the earliest picnics in England were medieval hunting feasts… Foods consumed would have been pastries, hams, baked meats and so on…' *Larousse Gastronomique* states that in Victorian Britain 'picnics may not have been as formal as country-house dinners, but they were often elaborate affairs [and] weekend shooting parties and sporting events were occasions for grand picnics, with extensive menus and elaborate presentation'. Mrs Beeton, in her famous book of household management, suggested that the contents of a hamper eminently suitable for a typical shooting party taking lunch outdoors should consist of such treats as lobsters, ribs of beef, roast chickens, a small ham, veal and ham pie, salads, fruit tarts, jellies, bread,

OPPOSITE TOP IN LORD RIPON'S TIME, LENGTHY LUNCHES WERE OFTEN TAKEN IN SPECIALLY ERECTED MARQUEES, SUCH AS CAN BE SEEN BEHIND THE LINE-UP OF GUNS, KEEPERS AND THEIR DOGS (COURTESY OF D. S. D. JONES)
OPPOSITE BELOW A LUNCH HUT CAN BE THE IDEAL PLACE TO DISPLAY MEMENTOES OF PREVIOUS SPORTING OCCASIONS

A SHOOTING PICNIC IN THIS DAY
AND AGE IS UNDOUBTEDLY A FAR
MORE SUBDUED AFFAIR THAN
THOSE OF EDWARDIAN TIMES
(COURTESY OF DAVID HUDSON)

HUNTING BRINGS MANY PLEASURES BUT GENERALLY, NOT MUCH LUNCH!
TRADITIONAL SANDWICH BOXES AFFIXED TO THE SADDLE ARE SELDOM LARGE ENOUGH
TO HOLD MUCH MORE THAN A ROUND OF SANDWICHES

Rachel Johnson, a contributor to the *Sunday Times*, sums up the likely lunch of Exmoor sportsmen and women in the following words: 'Exmoor is about hunting, shooting and fishing, and it's a place where a friend in tweed is a friend indeed... "eating out" means a pasty, to be ingested mid-hunt in three bites, before returning to the chase; it means a venison burger or a cheese sandwich – the ratio of cheddar to margarine must be even – ham sandwiches, mini-pasties or sausage rolls, a packet of crisps and a flask of tea.'

◆

fellow hunt followers had a purpose-made sandwich box strapped to their saddles which protected their chosen food very well indeed. But there's a great deal of difference between shooting and hunting: as we've seen, the shoot lunch is an important part of the day, whereas refreshment whilst out hunting is for sustenance only – hence the very valid comment made by Peter Holt when, in his introduction to *The Keen Shot's Miscellany*, he claimed 'I would have liked to have added a dedication to my wife Sarah but frankly it would have fallen on stony ground. A keen hunting person, an MFH indeed, she finds the idea of shooting faintly ridiculous. I retaliate by telling her that my idea of purgatory is the thought of six hours in the saddle without lunch.'

## *The Ultimate Steak Sandwich*

There are many variations on this classic; Jennifer Paterson and Clarissa Dickson Wright described it as a Shooter's Sandwich in their book *Two Fat Ladies*. (Apparently it was mentioned in the 1932 title *The Dinner Knell*, by T. Earle Welby.)

---

1 large steak, roughly the size of the length of a sandwich loaf
115g/4oz mushrooms, wiped and sliced
knob of butter
salt and pepper
1 sandwich loaf, uncut

---

Grill or fry the steak medium-rare, and fry the chopped mushrooms in the butter. Cut off the end of the loaf, removing as much crumb from the centre as is necessary to allow the steak to be slid into it and then pack in the mushrooms around the steak. Put back the crust and then wrap the loaf in blotting paper (if you can get it) before further wrapping in greaseproof paper and foil and tie into a neat parcel with string. Place under a weighted board for at least six hours and do not cut until needed.

## *Sausage and Brioche Loaf*

Similar in idea to the *Ultimate Steak Sandwich* is this recipe for Morteau sausage in brioche. The *saucisse de Morteau* is produced in the mountains and plateaus of France's Jura region, and is a pork sausage smoked over beech chips for 48 hours in *tuyés* – immense conical hearths – to give it a highly distinctive taste and aroma. Fortunately it's not necessary to travel to France to buy them as they are available in many UK delicatessens and online. This recipe comes from Ludovic Barbier; a keen shooting man and owner of *La Promenade*, a hotel and restaurant at Pont-de-Roide, in the Doubs area of France. It will, according to Ludovic, cut into six thick slices.

---

1 Morteau sausage
3 eggs
225g/8oz plain flour
1 sachet yeast
1 x 125ml wine glass crème fraîche
2 pinches salt
2 shallots, peeled and finely chopped
butter for frying

---

Pre-heat the oven to gas mark 2/150°C. Bake the sausage in its own juices for perhaps 45 minutes or until obviously cooked. Fry the shallots in the butter. Beat the eggs with the salt. Add the crème fraîche and mix well. Incorporate the flour and yeast. Grease a loaf tin and pour in approximately half the mixture – which should be thick enough to allow you to lay in the sausage without it disappearing to the bottom of the tin – add the shallots as you would in a hot dog and then cover with the rest of the egg/crème fraîche/flour mix and cook the loaf for 40 minutes. Allow to cool on a wire tray and slice when cold.

## Ham, Tomato and Avocado Sandwich

To jolly up a ham and tomato sandwich, try spooning out the flesh from a just-ripe avocado and gently mashing it with lemon juice and a dusting of freshly ground black pepper before adding it to the ham and tomato filling. It is absolutely delicious, especially on brown bread.

Burrito wraps also make an interesting alternative to using bread; they can be filled with any sort of mixture. Roll them up and store in tinfoil with the ends twisted like Christmas crackers until needed. Likewise, pitta bread pockets make a change from a conventional loaf.

## Chicken and Bacon with Avocado Mayonnaise

*For eight sandwiches use:*
1 large avocado
115ml/4fl oz mayonnaise
16 slices thick-cut granary bread
8 rashers cooked bacon
4 cooked chicken breast fillets
a little fresh dill
salt and black pepper

Halve the avocado, remove the stone and scoop out as much of the flesh as you can. In a basin, mix it well with the mayonnaise and add salt and pepper to taste. Spread the mixture evenly over all the slices of bread.

Slice each of the chicken breasts in half horizontally and, using a pair of scissors, chop the bacon rashers. Sprinkle a few bacon pieces onto a slice of bread and then place a half chicken breast on top. Sprinkle a little fresh dill over the chicken and cover with another slice of bread before cutting the sandwich in half. Wrap in clingfilm or kitchen foil until lunchtime.

## PIES AND PASTIES

As Sheila Hutchins noted in her book *Pâtés & Terrines*, raised pies containing all manner of meat – perhaps goose, capercaillie or York ham, stuffed with tongue, truffles and the like – were originally very elaborate and have been a speciality of the hunting shires for many years. Their history goes back even earlier than that, right back to the Middle Ages in fact, when the citizens of London used to buy them from vendors at Pye Corner. Pies appear in the writings of Chaucer and, of course, in the nursery rhyme 'Simple Simon', who famously 'met a pie-man going to the fair'. Henry Mayhew, writing in *London Labour and the London Poor* in 1851 mentioned that:

'The itinerant trade in pies is one of the most ancient street callings of London. The meat pies are made of beef or mutton; the fish pies of eels; the fruit of apples, currants, gooseberries… At the public houses a few pies are sold, and the pie-man makes a practice of looking in at all the taverns on his way. Here his customers are found principally in the tap-room. "Here's all 'ot!" the pie-man cries as he walks in. "Toss or buy! Up and win 'em!" This is the only way that the pies can be got rid of: "If it wasn't for tossing we shouldn't sell one". To "toss the pie-man" is a favourite pastime with costermongers' boys and all that class; some of whom aspire to the repute of being gourmands, and are critical of the quality of the comestible. If the pie-man wins the toss, he receives 1d. without giving a pie: if he loses, he hands it over for nothing. "Gentlemen out on the spree at the late public houses will frequently toss when they don't want the pies, and when they win they will amuse themselves by throwing the pies at one another, or at me."'

## *Shoot Day Pasties*

Jill Knowles, a lively and ebullient campaigner for the use of game produced as a result of shooting days, was kind enough to supply this recipe for a filling shoot day pasty.

---

puff pastry sheet

1 egg, beaten, to glaze

55g/2oz potato, diced

55g/2oz swede, diced

55g/2oz carrot, diced

55g/2oz onion, chopped

a good pinch fresh thyme, finely chopped

salt and pepper

1 pheasant breast

---

(The quantities of meat / vegetables given are sufficient to make one large pasty.)

Place the diced vegetables in a saucepan, cover with water. Bring to the boil and simmer for three minutes to soften and then drain. Roll out the pastry and cut into 12.5cm/5in rounds. Chop the raw pheasant breast into small pieces, add to the vegetables and mix together.

Fill half of each pastry round with the mixture. Glaze each edge with egg wash, fold over the filling, seal the edges and glaze the outside of the pasty with egg wash. Cook at gas mark 5/180°C for about 20 minutes or until the pastry is golden brown in colour.

Dr Johnson, who was born at the beginning of the eighteenth century, most obviously had a way with words – he did after all, produce one of the first official dictionaries – and therein defined 'nunchion' as being a 'piece of victuals eaten between meals' and 'lunch or luncheon' as being 'as much food as one's hand can hold' – surely then a sandwich? It was, of course, the 4th Earl of Sandwich who, according to popular belief, developed the idea of an immediate meal in the hand as a result of his gambling addiction whereby, reluctant though he may have been to leave the gaming table, he nevertheless required sustenance.

◆

## Mushroom and Chicken Puff Pastry Triangles

Attend a little shoot in the Trough of Bowland run by Peter and Richard Chambers and you might be offered these pastries made by Peter's wife Jenny, who says the quantities given here are sufficient to make eight. Jenny also remarked, as have so many other people in connection with *The Shoot Lunch*, 'I never bother to make my own puff pastry these days. Supermarket-bought is so easy to use and I defy anyone to tell the difference between that and home-made once it's got a tasty filling included.'

175g/6oz button mushrooms
75g/3oz butter
55g/2oz plain flour
225ml/8fl oz game or chicken stock
1 tablespoon sherry
salt and pepper
225g/8oz cooked chicken breasts, roughly chopped
75g/3oz frozen peas
1 egg
1 tablespoon milk
450g/1lb puff pastry

**OPPOSITE** APPETISING MEAT PIES AT RIPLEY CASTLE
(COURTESY OF TIM HARDY AND FRANK BODDY)

In 1826, at the Quarter Sessions held at Lostwithiel, Cornwall, farm labourer Philip Floyd was indicted for taking a pasty and linen cloth valued at 6d (2½p), the property of Richard Osborne and was imprisoned for 14 days in Bodmin Gaol. I hope it was a good pasty and the prison sentence worthwhile!

Sauté the mushrooms in about a third of the butter in a saucepan. Remove from the heat; spoon out the mushrooms with a slotted spoon and set to one side. Melt the remaining butter in the pan and then gently add the flour before returning to the heat and cooking, stirring all the time, for about two minutes. Add the stock and sherry and season to taste. Bring to the boil and simmer gently ('still stirring' says Jenny) until the sauce has thickened; probably a further two minutes. Stir in the chicken pieces, mushrooms and peas.

Beat together the egg and milk. Roll out half the pastry on a lightly floured board to make a square about 25–30cm/10–12in across. Cut the square of pastry into quarters and then take one of the squares and brush all four edges with the egg/milk mix. Spoon roughly one-eighth of the chicken mixture into the centre of the square before folding it into a triangle and sealing the edges between thumb and forefinger. Place on a greased and floured, or parchmented, baking sheet. Make up the other three squares in exactly the same way before then repeating the whole process with the other half of the puff pastry. Brush the tops of all eight triangles with whatever is left of the egg/milk mix and place in the oven to bake at gas mark 5/190ºC for 15–20 minutes or until golden brown.

## A Solo Affair

Some sporting days are perhaps best enjoyed without any human company – at least in the minds of certain aficionados. Pigeon flighting, ferreting or fishing are good examples, as might be a trip out with a pointing dog and a hawk. An article in *The Independent* once commented, 'Falconry enjoys a glamour that appeals to all romantics. It is the oldest and the noblest of all country sports, practised for four thousand years'. Unfortunately, apart from possibly during medieval times when lunch would have been a prominent part of the day, provisions do not nowadays reflect the sport's glamour and lunch will, like days spent on horseback in the hunting field, most likely be a simple sandwich or pie eaten whenever a natural break permits. Having said that, I note that there is at least one person offering a day's hawking experience to the interested tyro who promises participants 'lunch in the woods' courtesy of his hunting Harris hawks: 'they do the catching and I do the cooking'!

## Pesky Midges

Any attempt at outdoor eating whilst shooting or stalking in the Scottish Highlands is likely to be in the company of midges, especially in August. So great a problem are they that a mini-industry has developed around the manufacture and supply of all manner of chemical

WOULD-BE SPECTATORS AND PARTICIPANTS AT A FIELD TRIAL MIGHT BE HORRIFIED
TO LEARN THAT NOT ALL ORGANISERS AND JUDGES STOP FOR AN OFFICIAL LUNCH BREAK!
(COURTESY OF DAVID HUDSON)

and herbal deterrents. Ideas as to how to rid oneself of the attention of midges range from the technical to those of the 'old wives' tale' variety.

First appearing about ten years ago, a small gadget became available which was powered by propane and emitted a thin, moist plume of carbon dioxide intended to mimic the exhalation of hot-blooded animals. This was then flavoured with Octenol, a chemical compound which, according to Ben Macintyre writing in *The Times* in August 2002, 'is barely perceptible to man but foie gras to a midge'. (The makers of Octenol claimed that it was a 'naturally occurring by-product that comes from some animals such as cattle, which ingest large amounts of vegetable matter.') Macintyre then went on to explain that, 'lured by the illusion there is a vast, heavy-breathing cow in the vicinity, the female midges swarm towards the source, where they are sucked by vacuum into a mesh bag and then perish'.

A report in *The Scotsman* (3 September 1985) described a far simpler solution, which was to take strong vitamin C tablets of 200–250mg before venturing out. Apparently several amateur experiments had been tried and 'it works splendidly' claimed the article. Similar success has been claimed for the B vitamins, especially vitamin B1 (thiamine).

As far as old wives' cures are concerned, they range from the well-known but unfortunately erroneous idea that the smoke from cigarettes or cigars will keep them away, to eating copious amounts of Marmite, which once exuded through the pores of the skin, midges find repulsive. (Marmite, of course, contains vitamin B1.) At one time, Highland gypsies used to soak their neckties in paraffin – I sincerely hope they didn't then try the lit-cigarette method as back-up!

Alasdair Roberts, writing in his wonderful little book simply entitled *Midges* tells us that the word 'midge' derives from Old Norse *muggia*, so it is perhaps no surprise that the oldest folk remedy is mugwort (*Artemisia vulgaris*). Midge problems in the Scottish Highlands are not new to the sportsman. Writing in 1860, fisherman Charles Weld remarked:

'Talk of solitude on the moors! Why, every square yard contains a population of millions of these little harpies, that pump blood out of you with amazing savageness and insatiability. Where they come from is a puzzle. While you are in motion not one is visible, but when you stop a mist seems to curl about your feet and legs rising and at the same time expanding, until you become painfully sensible that the appearance is due to a cloud of gnats. When seven miles from Scourie I came to the Laxford, a glorious salmon river spanned by a bridge, backed by Ben Stack and framed by rocks, garlanded by fern and birch… I had no longer sat down than up rose millions of midges, which sent me reeling down the craggy steep, half mad.'

## A Shoot Punch

Depending on where you eat your lunch on the go, there might just be the facilities and opportunity to make up a warming punch for everyone to enjoy on the coldest of days or at the pre-Christmas shoot. This punch should be served hot and will fill 12–15 average-sized goblets.

1 orange, stuck with cloves
2 bottles claret
1 lemon, sliced
55g/2oz blanched whole almonds
55g/2oz raisins
115g/4oz sugar
a cinnamon stick
115ml/4fl oz brandy

Bake the orange in a moderate oven for about an hour. Meanwhile, put the bottles of wine, the lemon, cinnamon stick, almonds, raisins and half the quantity of sugar into a large saucepan. Add the orange when baked and simmer the pan uncovered for 15 minutes.

In a small pan, place the remaining sugar and the brandy. Heat very gently, ignite with a match and, whilst still flaming, pour gently and carefully into the punch. Serve straight away.

# Feeding a Crowd

The inclusion of this chapter is not intended to suggest any form of distinction between those who shoot and those who ensure that a shooting day is successful. Instead, it is designed to discuss those occasions when Guns, beaters and pickers-up join together to 'feed at the same trough' and to give a few suggestions as to how best and simplest to feed what, on the large shoot, might well end up being a very big team indeed. There are also close season occasions when Guns and shooting syndicates may get together, for example, for a summer clay shoot, at which a barbeque could be included.

The history of catering for large numbers of people at a sporting lunch has already been described in the first chapter of this book, but it is worth reminding ourselves of the vast quantities and varieties of food provided in times gone by. There was, for example, the occasion in 1618 when the Earl of Mar

**OPPOSITE TOP** GUNS AND BEATERS ON THE LYBURN SHOOT, HAMPSHIRE, EAT A HOT MEAL DESPITE A LACK OF ELECTRICITY AND MODERN AMENITIES (COURTESY OF TONY MOSS)
**OPPOSITE BELOW** A SLOVENIAN BARBEQUE WHICH IS USED DURING THE SEASON BY LOCAL SHOOTING PARTIES

hosted a hunting and hawking party and, according to one guest who wrote of the occasion afterwards, provided them with an almost unbelievable feast:

'The kitchen was on the side of a bank, many kettles and pots boiling, and many spits turning and winding, with great varieties of cheer, such as venison, baked, boiled, or roast; and stewed beef, mutton, goats, kids, hares, fresh salmon, pigeons, hens, capons, chickens, partridges, cootes [sic], heath-cocks, capercaillies, and ptarmigans; good ale, sherry, white wine, claret, sweet red, and most potent spirits.'

To return to the present day, mention must be made of the complaint often levelled at the Guns by beaters who ask if it is really necessary for the shooting party to spend so long over lunch whilst they themselves are getting bored and cold waiting for the Guns to come out again afterwards. The short answer is that a good keeper or whoever is in charge of the beating line will usefully utilise both the mid-morning break and the lunchtime session in order to blank in a few out-of-the way parts of the shooting ground, and otherwise prepare for the next drive.

Len Macey, quoted by Brian Martin in *Tales of the Old Gamekeepers*, had this to say: '… keepers and beaters always had to be away smartly to sort out the blanking in: much as it is today really, though any good shoot captain always ensures the Guns are on parade at the right time.' Easier said than done perhaps – as I know from personal experience that Guns cannot always be hurried after lunch even though they know there is still more sport to be enjoyed. Mr Macey is right in what he says though; it is important to have everyone on their pegs at the appointed time, especially if birds have been blanked some considerable distance and are keen to get home: if one bird panics and flies, the others around it will soon follow – and there is nothing more galling to the keeper and beaters to see streams of birds flying well over empty gun pegs! For their part then, Guns should make every effort to ensure that they are back on their pegs at the time agreed.

## STEWS AND CASSEROLES

Some crusty French bread is an essential accompaniment to both stews and casseroles, the most popular way of feeding large quantities of hungry outdoor types. Such dishes can be prepared the day before and then either reheated in situ at the lunch venue or at home prior to being brought out at the last minute.

OPPOSITE BEATERS AND STOPS OFTEN LEAVE BEFORE THE GUNS HAVE FINISHED LUNCH IN ORDER TO BLANK IN AND PREPARE FOR THE NEXT DRIVE

— 118 —

'YOU CAN'T GO WRONG WITH A STEW!'

Mark Munday is the head keeper at the Hollycombe estate in Liphook, Hampshire, and his partner Jane often makes a huge stew for the beaters and pickers-up. Jane says that she caters for between thirty and forty people, preparing and part-cooking the food the day before it is required. She comments that, 'it is difficult to be precise with any recipe as I do just guess… but you can't really go too far wrong with a stew!' For those reasons the main base of the stew is eight packs of casserole beef, a five-kilo bag of potatoes, six large onions, six to eight leeks and five packs of diced carrot and swede. Jane continues: 'I used to peel and dice them myself and then Sainsbury's started selling packs already done… what a time saver!'

Optional ingredients include tins of haricot beans, lentils, frozen peas and copious amounts of concentrated beef stock. Everything is put into a very large stewpot then covered with water and brought to the boil, before the heat is turned down and the contents simmered for about two and a half hours. The next day Jane reheats the stew for a further four hours and then, in order to further thicken it, makes up a mixture of approximately six beef and six vegetable Oxo cubes, eight tablespoons of plain flour and eight tablespoons of Bisto (all of which is mixed with a little water until a thick yet creamy consistency is achieved). This is gradually added to the stew about half an hour before serving and requires constant stirring in order to prevent any lumpiness (the stew must be bubbling/boiling when this is done).

Lancashire Hotpot is a very traditional and filling dish after which no one goes away hungry! This suggestion comes from Lancashire-based Michelle Butterworth who makes hers on top of an Aga nicknamed 'Cromwell'. Traditionally made with lamb, everyone's recipe for this dish is, however, a little different and one shooting lunch enthusiast suggests that it should always be made with mutton, which, according to him, has 'so much more flavour' but is not always easy to find these days. In one of her books, Clarissa Dickson-Wright even suggests adding some fresh oysters to the hotpot.

Elizabeth Ainley, who cooks for a team of Guns and beaters at the Barwick Shoot in Warwickshire, says that she usually has to cater for around twenty-five people and, in the interests of economy, almost always uses minced beef in her menu. 'No one seems to mind whether it's in shepherd's pie or chilli con carne. The main thing seems to be that there's plenty of it! Sometimes I serve chilli as a filling for baked potatoes and other times with rice.' Barwick Shoot members and helpers have their lunch in what shoot captain James Ledbetter describes as a 'centrally-heated Crystal Palace'. It is, apparently, a disused commercial greenhouse, the heating system of which one of the syndicate has adapted for use with a log-burning stove bought for fifty pounds from a local scrap merchant.

I have, over the years, acquired quite a collection of books to do with hunting and shooting. At one time I used to buy anything and everything before I realised that, even in second-hand bookshops, as opposed to antiquarian ones, I was spending a lot of money – so I decided to restrict myself to books published before 1950. Many, especially the hunting ones, dated from between the wars. My collection was given a boost in the late 1980s when a local aged and much respected sportsman died, and his wife invited me to take as many books as I wanted from his library. A sense of decorum meant that I shouldn't be greedy so I restricted myself to fifteen rather than the fifty or so I would really have liked! In one, there happened to be a typed recipe for Country Casserole (the book was actually written by A. G. Street, my all-time favourite country writer who was not, to my knowledge, known for his culinary skills!). In pencil, in the margin, is the comment, 'this is very good and feeds sixteen'. Whoever wrote the comment and when they did so, I have no idea!

IN PLACES WHERE LUNCH IS
NOT PROVIDED, MOST MAKE DO
WITH SANDWICHES AND A FLASK
(COURTESY OF TONY MOSS)

cannot do an afternoon drive on an empty stomach", a choice hare paté sandwich, he puts all the skill born of long practice into his nonchalant "Oh well, just one". After that, because Reggie's not a bad chap, all combine to save him the embarrassment of noticing that by the end of the lunch what has been offered all round has added up to a hearty meal.'

## PUDDNGS AND POCKET-FILLERS

A main meal is normally all that is expected in the beaters' shed, but there are some shoots catering for large numbers who will offer everyone a doughnut or two, a slab of fruit cake or cheese and biscuits. It is probably better just to supply one or two cheeses rather than a selection – and you cannot go too far wrong with a truckle of good quality Cheddar.

One of the great advantages of such 'finger food' is the fact that, when the keeper comes in and demands that all the beaters be on the trailer in one minute flat, a handful of such food is easily grabbed in the mad panic that will inevitably ensue! For the same reason, it is not a bad idea to have ready a bowl of individual chocolate bars.

On the subject of chocolates after lunch, an internet shooting forum has an interesting posting from a regular beater: 'We had the most super Beaters' Day at our shoot. The atmosphere was terrific, masses of birds, good laughs in the beaters' wagon, mad dogs, sloe gin, fast gin, any amount of best port... best of all we had Chilli-Chocolate Sweets! A lovely tin of well-wrapped Roses chocolates was passed around after soup. The flavour was surprising, but they went down a treat. They are made by injecting strong chilli sauce, with a syringe, through the wrapping paper. They are sensational.'

## THE END-OF-SEASON DINNER

An end of season beaters' dinner is always a good idea. It is evidently not a new thing as, back in 1909, Owen Jones described the beaters' supper as being 'an excellent institution, and, punctuated by judicious speeches, goes a long way to weld together those bonds of sporting sympathy which are so vital to the best interests of shooting. Even if you cannot afford the menu of a City company, you can run to rabbit pie, than which, washed down with British beer, there is nothing more to the taste of the British beater'.

Jones was, to my mind, absolutely correct in his thinking and there is nothing more likely to engender camaraderie amongst the beating team than a shoot dinner – perhaps held on the evening of the last shooting day. If there are enough volunteers (perhaps everyone could bring a plate of food?) and there is a suitable shoot hut or warm outbuilding, it could be run along the lines of a traditional harvest supper. More likely at that time of year, it may be better to make arrangements with the manager or owner of the local pub, who will most likely be only too pleased to accommodate a large party of people at the end of a month which is normally quiet after the excesses of Christmas and the New Year. Use that point (as well as the fact that there should be a discount for numbers) in your negotiations! The most usual way of doing things is to have a roast main meal followed by a pudding – though some places may offer a choice of menu to the diners, but if not, most people are happy with beef followed by apple pie, for example.

There then arises the thorny question of who will pay for it all. Some shoot owners are quite prepared to do this or at least subsidise the meal part of the evening (most are, however, understandably cautious about agreeing to pay for the whole bar bill) but if not, the beating team might agree to pay for their meal with their wages from the last beating day. One shoot I know used to have a beaters' sweepstake on each day's bag throughout the season but whoever won only ever received half of the total; the remaining half went into a kitty which then more or less financed the end-of-season dinner.

Apparently, in some parts of Kent and Sussex, St Andrew's Day (30 November) was once a traditional day for squirrel hunting. Youths and young men went out armed with sticks, clubs and sometimes guns, and, according to a certain E. Hasted, writing in the second volume of *The History and Topographical Survey of Kent* in 1782, often killed more than just squirrels: 'The labourers and lower kind of people spend the greatest part of the day in parading through the woods and grounds, with loud shoutings; and under the pretence of demolishing the squirrels, some few of which they kill, they destroy numbers of hares, pheasants, partridges, and in short, whatever comes their way, breaking down hedges and doing much other mischief, and in the evening betaking themselves to the ale-houses, finish their career there as is usual with such sort of gentry.' I think we might take it that E. Hasted did not approve!

◆

It is usual at such events to incorporate a few speeches – some of which might even be serious – and possibly even a prize-giving, for the person who has fallen most times into the ditch, whose dog has run in the most, and a whole host of other spurious awards. The 'prizes' should obviously reflect the humour of the occasion.

## SUMMER CLAY SHOOTS AND BARBEQUES

I am a great advocate of planning an out-of-season get-together in order that Guns and beaters continue to feel involved with the shoot during the summer months. One of the most effective ways of doing this is to organise a clay shoot and barbeque on a suitable piece of land well away from where newly released game is likely to be found. The summer barbeque is then, another form of shooting lunch and, as such, deserves brief mention here.

### *Lighting the barbeque*

It is a good fire-base that ensures the success or otherwise of a barbequed meal – cooking over an open fire only gives raw meat a singed surface, whereas charcoal burning grey but shot with a reddish glow will give a constant heat and evenly cooked food. Use only as much

charcoal as is required: there is often a tendency to totally fill the bottom of the barbeque, but this is not necessary unless a very large cooking surface is required.

Light the barbeque well in advance of the time that you wish to begin cooking – depending on the wind conditions and the likely draught, an hour ahead is not too early. The heat should be even and glowing before you even think to begin cooking. Low heat can be gained by spacing out the charcoal and a hot one by flicking away the white ash from the top of the charcoal. Always add extra fuel from the edge of the fire rather than tipping it on top of the already burning charcoal, and if unwanted flames occur as a result of dripping fat, use a fine water spray to keep them doused.

## How long to barbeque?

A beef steak of average thickness should be given between 4–10 minutes on each side depending on whether it is required rare or well done. It should be cooked over a hot flame, unlike pork chops which are normally cooked from 15–25 minutes each side over a low to medium heat. Gammon slices can be done in the same way but the length of time per side is reduced to 5–8 minutes, depending on the thickness. Lamb chops are cooked over a medium flame for

6–10 minutes to be rare to medium-rare whilst chicken joints also need a medium heat and a longer cooking time of between 15–30 minutes. It is, however, most important to ensure that chicken is cooked right the way through in order to avoid any possible danger of salmonella.

If you are lucky there might be someone connected with the shoot who has access to a source of trout. After the fish have been gutted and cleaned, their sides should be gently scored every inch or so with a sharp knife. These cuts can then be rubbed with a mix of fresh herbs and/or spices before the fish is liberally coated with olive oil and lime juice. Finally, rub in some sea salt before laying the trout over white-burning charcoal and leaving for a couple of minutes before gently lifting them from the grill in order to ensure that they are not sticking and that the skin and flesh facing the heat is not black. Keep turning from side to side until cooked – a very rough guide, depending on the heat would be between 10 and 15 minutes for a 450g/1lb fish.

## Barbeque accompaniments

Bowls of crisp lettuce leaves, whole tomatoes, chunks of cucumber, dishes of sliced beetroot, jars of chutney and various dressings are all usual barbeque accompaniments but what about new potatoes, rice and pasta? Also, the famous diarist John Evelyn suggested even as far back as 1699 that you should include cress and fennel to mushrooms, young nettles and wood sorrel for a 'sallet'. The Romans had a salad speciality of rose petals, brains and eggs (interesting!) and ate cucumbers or endives dressed with liquamen – a fish dressing – and lettuce infused with wine vinegar spiced with ginger and cumin. They were in this respect, as with many other things, way ahead of their time. For drinks, perhaps offer spritzers, wine, Pimms, beer or cider, plus plenty of mineral water and juices.

An extract from W. Bromley-Davenport's *Sport*, published in 1888:

'A noble lord, a distinguished cavalry officer and an awful martinet, had a large shooting party, when, in spite of endless loudly-given orders, marching, and counter-marching of beaters, everything seemed to go wrong, pheasants included. So at the end of a covert in which little had been found, and that little not properly "brought to the gun", the head keeper was summoned, and, all resplendent in green and gold as he was, advanced with abject mien, faltering some trembling excuses to his by now almost rabid master, who, cutting these sternly short, asked: "Shall we find more in the next covert?" "I hope so, my lord." "*Hope*, sir!" roared the peer with terrific emphasis on the verb. "Do you think I give you a hundred pounds a year to *hope*? Now, go and beat that wood this way, and I'll post the guns." "Your lordship means this wood?" said the terrified functionary, pointing to another. "No, I don't." "But my lord..." expostulated the man, now more alarmed than ever. "Not a word, sir, obey orders!" Irresolute, and evidently much perplexed, the wretched man marched off with his army and beat the wood, in which there was absolutely nothing. Terrible then to see the wrath of the baffled soldier, till the miserable keeper, seeing he was about to be dismissed on the spot, cried out in heart-rending accents: "It's not your wood, my lord. It belongs to Lord W" (his neighbour) "and he shot it last Friday!" All the keepers and beaters knew this, yet not one had dared to gainsay Achilles in his ire.'

SAUSAGES – THE STAPLE OF
ALMOST EVERY BARBEQUE!

# Wine, Coffee and Cigars

Richard Jefferies's main character in *The Gamekeeper at Home* (first published as a series of articles in 1878) claimed that while he hadn't signed the pledge, he wasn't too fussed about partaking of alcohol: '… if a man asks me to take a glass of ale, I never says him no. But I ain't got no barrel at home… Gentlemen gives me tips – of course they does; and much obliged I be; but I takes it to my missus. Many's the time they've axed me to have a glass of champagne or brandy when we've had lunch under the hedge; but I always says no…' Such observations notwithstanding, it is often the weather that dictates what people would like to drink at lunchtime. I have been ready to serve a Bloody Mary, only to find that on a mild, late October day the Guns, clad in shirtsleeves and shooting vests, have an eye on a cold beer.

**OPPOSITE TOP** COFFEE FROM A FILTER MACHINE IS ARGUABLY THE BEST OPTION FOR A SHOOTING LUNCH
**BELOW LEFT** A SMALL CUBAN CIGAR IN THE HAND BUILDS UP A FUG IN THE BUSH DURING THE MID-MORNING BREAK

There are as many ways of making a Bloody Mary as there are people who make them, so I usually place all the ingredients on the bar top and try to get Guns to make their own! (Some say that the easiest way to make a Bloody Mary is to use Big Tom or other spiced tomato juice and thereby do away with all the stirring and mixing: it is certainly an option worth considering.)

## Mixing a Bloody Mary

When mixing a Bloody Mary from scratch, I find that the following method and quantities will make enough for a team of eight Guns: I put everything in a jug and only add ice once the mix has been poured into individual glasses.

---

850ml/1½pts tomato juice
300ml/½pt vodka
60ml/2fl oz Lea & Perrins Worcestershire sauce
60ml/2fl oz lemon juice
a dozen drops of Tabasco
1 teaspoon each of salt and freshly ground black pepper

---

## A 'Virgin Mary'

To make a 'Virgin Mary' (although some might ask what's the point!), you could of course, simply omit the vodka from the above recipe and let those who want it add their own; however, if you prefer to be a bit more conscientious about making the perfect glass, gather together:

---

a wedge of lemon
1 heaped teaspoon celery salt
1 level teaspoon freshly ground black pepper
ice cubes
125ml/4fl oz tomato juice
1 tablespoon lemon juice
1 teaspoon Lea & Perrins Worcestershire sauce
1 drop Tabasco sauce

---

Wipe the lemon wedge around the rim of a glass and dip the rim into the combined salt and pepper. Half fill a cocktail shaker with the ice and add the tomato juice, lemon juice, Lea & Perrins and Tabasco sauce and shake well before pouring the contents into the glass.

## Sorry, there's a fee to pay before we can deliver your item

**REF:**

# 10612 – SU

SURNAME: Yeomans
ADDRESS: Pump Cottage
Bath Road, Easting, STONEHOUSE
POSTCODE: GL10 3AX    DATE BOOKED: 08/05/2024
REASON: THE SENDER DID NOT PAY THE FULL POSTAGE
AMOUNT DUE: £ 1.50

**Royal Mail**

Ref No.

☐ Signature item

Amount Due includes a handling fee. See royalmail.com/feetopay for details

*All postal items entering the UK may be assessed by HMRC and may incur charges. Any package liable for VAT/customs duties, will also incur a Royal Mail handling fee of £8. For more information on customs charges please visit **gov.uk** and search for **Notice 143**.

## What to do next?

➤ Visit **royalmail.com/feetopay** to choose a delivery day

➤ Simply pay with PayPal, or a Credit or Debit Card

**Can't pay online?**
Paying online gives you the flexibility to select a convenient day for delivery, but we understand it isn't always an option. In these cases, you can pay:
**With postage** – Add stamps or a franking machine impression overleaf for the Amount Due. Post this card and we'll deliver your item.
**In person** – Bring this card and payment to the address overleaf. Please also bring proof of your identity: Passport, driving licence, credit/debit card or cheque book.

**Please note: we will keep underpaid items for 18 calendar days and Customs items for 21 calendar days, before returning to sender.**

P4605 March 2021. Royal Mail is a trading name of Royal Mail Group Ltd. Registered in England and Wales. Registered number 4138203 . Registered office 185 Farringdon Road, London, EC1A 1AA.

ite Burgundy; Cru ally, I quite like the e Saumur end of the asant and fruity and ranschhoek are easily

d virtually all of them s to their temperature,

In some shooting lunch dining places, you might well see a tantalus on the sideboard – usually containing three decanters locked in a wooden frame. These were originally made as a way of keeping the household staff from helping themselves to their employer's pre-prandial drinks: a locking mechanism meant that the decanters could not be taken from the frame without the use of a key, which the master kept close to his person! One patent lock device was actually invented by George Betjeman, the great-grandfather of the late poet and Poet Laureate, Sir John Betjeman. The contrivance itself came by its name because Tantalus, a Greek god, was hung from the Tree of Life, but could not reach the fruit nor slake his thirst..

which you are ...... .....g .. a coffee-filter and periodically pour a little of the wine into the decanter via the funnel.

Red wine should be served in clear, quite large, rounded glasses. If they are tulip-shaped this will concentrate the bouquet, very much a plus point according to the aficionados.

CHAMPAGNE IS APPRECIATED AS
A PRE-LUNCH DRINK OR AT THE
MID-MORNING BREAK – IN FACT,
AS THE 1970s TV ADVERT FOR
MARTINI USED TO CLAIM, 'ANY
TIME, ANY PLACE, ANYWHERE!'
(COURTESY OF TIM HARDY
AND FRANK BODDY)

## *Which wine?*

Wines that go well with almost any shooting lunch include the likes of French wines such as Savigny, Chambolle-Musigny, Crozes Hermitage and Nuits St Georges; Italian Chianti Classico; Californian Pinot Noir and Australian Majella. Vicky Williams, of Berry Bros & Rudd (Britain's oldest wine and spirit merchant, having traded from the same shop in St James's Street, London, for over three hundred years) suggests that a light red wine well suited to the purpose would be Pinot Noir and further adds: 'This is also the perfect wine to suit all foods including white meat, red meat and even "meatier" fish dishes.' It is important not to dismiss the oaky white wines: some go well with autumnal foods and have a fullness that the likes of Sauvignon Blanc and other lighter styles cannot match.

If you are looking for something with a little more body (and generally at a higher price), try Côte Rôte, St Estephe or a Margaux. Personally, I am quite keen on Italian wines: try a Barolo or if you prefer a more lightweight Italian wine, comparable to the French Saumur Champigny or Fleurie, experiment with a Montepulciano d'Abruzzo. If you are looking for a Spanish wine, go for a Rioja, or anything from the Navarra region. Portuguese wines are also good. When asked for his personal selection that might suit a sporting lunch, writer and acknowledged wine buff Philippe de Randolph suggested 'any young Italian red; a Chinon, Chiroubles, Saumur Champigny, Fleurie, or even a rosé from the Rhone Valley'. If you are tempted towards a rosé, it is however, important to remember that it is the drier, rather than off-dry types that go best with food. These work extremely well with grilled pork chops or a pork roast.

A very valid point on the subject of suitable wines is that given the overall cost of a shoot, there is no reason to poison your guests with cheap plonk that has more in common with paraffin than good grapes.

## *Buying wine*

You can, of course, just nip down to your local supermarket and buy some very good wines that are ready to drink at any shooting lunch: they will be affordable and perfectly acceptable, but why not consider the possibility of buying wines to keep and mature? There are several reasons for doing so, the first and most sensible being that, whilst good quality mature wines can be bought, they are generally quite expensive; whereas if you buy the same wine not long after it has been bottled and is first released onto the market (*en primeur*), it can be obtained at a fraction of the price.

**OPPOSITE**
CHAMPAGNE AND WHITE WINES ARE, OF COURSE, GENERALLY SERVED CHILLED

When you are buying wines to keep, arguably the best place to do so is at a specialist wine merchant. If you pick the right one and tell them exactly what you are looking for (and, most importantly, how much you can afford to spend), they will be only too pleased to guide you through the process. Who knows, they might even open a few bottles and let you try before you buy. Once you've gained a little experience, you might try buying your wine online or by mail order: in fact, it might even be worthwhile becoming a member of a wine club. Wine clubs are a good way of trying the many different wine types and once you've come across something you know is likely to go well with a typical shoot lunch, you can seek out a supplier in order to buy a couple of cases.

## *Tips for storage*

Traditionally, bottles of wine are stored on their sides to ensure that the corks do not dry out. If, like most of us, you are not in the happy situation of having a specially constructed cellar, always choose a dark area as your storage place, and keep the bottles well away from anything which may cause the wine to become tainted as a result of an unwanted taste being introduced through the porous cork. The garden shed might be good in that it is cool and dark, though it would be a shame if your wine tastes of over-wintered garlic or lawn-mower petrol as a result of sharing the same space! The ideal temperature for storing (not serving – which is a totally different topic) wine is anywhere between 6–14°C and, if you want to get technical, should have a humidity rating of between 55 and 75 percent – so keep your wine well away from your central heating boiler. Also avoid storing it in the utility room next to the washing machine or tumble dryer because the resultant vibrations will be continually stirring up any sediment. Often the cupboard under the stairs is your best bet.

## NON-ALCOHOLIC ALTERNATIVES

It is important to remember that not everyone drinks alcohol. Make sure that there are sufficient alternatives for those who don't (and always make sure that there is plenty of iced water, topped up with thick slices of lime for both the drinkers and non-drinkers).

Bizarrely, it would appear that some teas may go well with a shooting lunch and whilst the subject comes under greater discussion in the next chapter, it is well worth considering the thoughts of long-time tea enthusiast Alison Armes, who owns and manages Rosie & Java, a specialist tea and coffee merchants nestling in the lanes of Richmond-upon-Thames.

'Lapsang Souchong tea has a wonderfully intense smoky aroma and flavour. The flavour works well with roast chicken and English blue cheese such as Stilton. [A meal of] rich roast belly of pork, [is best when] finished with the exquisite Jasmine Pearl silver tea. Each pearl is hand-rolled and has the most intense jasmine flavour.

Silver tea is light, fresh and an aid to the digestion of the rich pork meat. Rich venison casserole cooked in red wine certainly deserves a rich red Kenya Broken Pekoe tea. Beautifully red and robust – like the deer – Kenya BP is also an ideal partner with rare roast beef. Flowering Art Tea is particularly suitable at the end of any meal; whether you are lunching on rich, light, or wholesome foods.'

## Coffee

For many of us, coffee or tea comes straight out of a flask on a shooting day and is, for convenience, either the instant or teabag variety. There are many rituals attached; some making their coffee with hot milk, others preferring it black straight from a flask. Tea drinkers too, can quite often be seen carrying out quite an elaborate ceremony of placing a teabag in the cup of the flask before then adding water from the flask and allowing it to steep for a certain length of time before finally adding just the right amount of milk from an unbreakable bottle kept specifically for the purpose. (More on tea can, by the way, be found in the following chapter, as I have already mentioned.)

The British Coffee Association suggests that coffee trees were first noticed in the province of Kaffa – today known as Ethiopia – and that they were subsequently grown in monastery gardens after a local abbot was told by a goat-herder that even his most mature animals appeared magically revitalised after eating the beans which fell from the tree. The abbot thought that a boiling of these into liquid form might keep his monks awake during their long periods of meditation – and so it proved.

Today there are many designs and varieties of coffee-makers but in the early nineteenth century, the usual way to make coffee was to pour hot water over coffee grounds in a pot. This of course meant that it was impossible to separate the muddy sludge from the liquid. According to the British Coffee Association, it was a certain Elizabeth Dakin who invented the coffee plunger (cafetière) so commonly in use today. She also felt that some metallic materials used in the construction of coffee roasters could 'impart noxious qualities' to the coffee and because of this, developed roasters made of gold, silver or platinum.

As coffee has to stand for periods of time throughout the shooting day, most notably in the morning when one is awaiting the arrival of guest Guns, it is as well to choose your coffee-maker carefully. Probably a filter machine is the type best suited to the

Eventually, the Dutch colonies became the main suppliers of coffee to Europe and, in London; many coffee-houses were opened during the seventeenth century. At the time, coffee houses were often called Penny Universities because of the cheap education they provided – for a fee of one penny, visitors could read the newspapers, listen to lectures and engage in discussion on any number of disparate topics. Indeed, the Royal Society is said to have sprung from one such venue and men like Edmund Halley (he of comet fame) were known to have met at Jonathan's Coffee House in Change Alley, in order to compare ideas. Interestingly, the site of that particular coffee house eventually became the home of the London Stock Exchange..

◆

shooting day. Always go for those that have paper filters: although permanent filters may save you money (and how much is it when compared with a day's shooting!), paper ones are far more hygienic and can simply be thrown away after use.

## *Coffees suitable for after lunch*

Robert Armes (coffee expert and husband of Alison at Rosie & Java) maintains that 'coffee to drink throughout lunch should be medium roast with a well balanced flavour'. He suggests trying medium roast Ethiopian Yirgacheffe: 'Yirgacheffe is light in colour when brewed but has an amazing clean, smooth and full-bodied flavour. Drink it with or without milk. Yirgacheffe is undoubtedly a coffee that you will always remember as being a wonderful drinking experience.'

Robert continues:

'After a meal a full, rich shot or two of Italian-style espresso is recommended. Pulled short with a thick golden "crema" top is the mark of a perfect shot. As the last drip hits the cup espresso must be drunk immediately before it dies. Within seconds that moment of ultimate pleasure will be lost! A fresh continental roast Monsoon Malabar bean is an excellent espresso brewing choice [as] the flavour lingers wonderfully on the palate always leaving you wanting more and wishing your espresso could last forever. For the ultimate decadent indulgence add a Cohiba Cuban cigar to enhance the experience!'

## CIGARS

For some inexplicable reason, several of us who are non-smokers on a day-to-day basis seem compelled to enjoy a cigar after a shooting lunch and, if it's a good one, can be seen still puffing away at it during the first drive of the afternoon. I thought it might be of interest to include a little information here regarding the lunchtime (and indeed, shooting day) smoke. Simon Chase, non-executive director of Hunters & Frankau – premier London cigar importers – made the following suggestions when I asked whether there might be such a thing as an ideal cigar to enjoy on a shooting day.

'I would suggest that you should start with a lighter flavoured Cuban brand such as Hoyo de Monterrey or H. Upmann for the morning coffee-break, in one of the popular, heavy gauge, robust sizes like the Hoyo Epicure No. 2 (4⅞in x 50 ring gauge)

OPPOSITE
FOR MANY, COFFEE OR TEA DRUNK ON A SHOOTING DAY COMES STRAIGHT FROM A THERMOS –
BEATER AND DOG ENJOYING A QUIET LUNCHTIME MOMENT

— 142 —

Understandably, the narrator of the following story was keen to draw a veil over the identity of the character at fault, but has nevertheless agreed to its inclusion!

'A friend of mine was shooting with a senior member of the Spanish Royal Family. In between drives, the Spaniard's cigar went out and he discovered that his lighter was empty. An ADC was dispatched to my friend's adjacent butt to borrow a lighter. My friend obliged with a cheap, throw-away device. The cigar was duly re-lit. Then, rather surprisingly, the regal Spaniard handed his gun to the ADC and walked determinedly over to my friend's butt with the lighter. He returned it and thanked him for it, but added that he should not have used it and would never use it again. Puzzled, my friend examined the lighter and saw written on it in large letters "Keep Gibraltar British".'

◆

or the H. Upmann Connoisseur No. 1 (5in by 48 ring gauge). After lunch you could move up to a slightly richer brand such as Romeo y Julieta, perhaps in the Short Churchill size (4⅞in x 50 ring gauge). In the afternoon, go to the fuller flavoured Ramon Allones Specially Selected (4⅞in x 50 ring gauge) and then after dinner (if your host likes you enough to invite you to stay!) try a large Partagas like the Lusitania (7⅝in x 49 ring gauge) or a Churchill size (7in x 47 ring gauge) from Cohiba, called the Esplendido, or perhaps one from Bolivar, where it is known as the Corona Gigante.

'There are, of course, plenty of small hand-made Cuban cigar sizes suitable for a twenty minute or so smoke. Like the Montecristo No. 5 or Cohiba Siglo I (4in x 40 ring gauge). A robusto size (4⅞in x 50 ring gauge) will take about 40 minutes to smoke and a Churchill about an hour.

'It is perhaps relevant to observe that the 47 ring gauge Churchill, which has a diameter of 47/64 of an inch or 0.73in has exactly the same girth as a 12-bore barrel and cartridge. Many Cuban cigars come in aluminium tubes, which are ideal for protecting their contents when one is out and about. As the girth of cigars resembles that of a 12 bore cartridge, these tubes can fit comfortably into a standard cartridge belt.'

It might be as well to mention here that the comparative sizes of a cartridge and a Churchill can result in some confusion, as shown in the story Hunters & Frankau's chairman, David Lewis, tells against himself: 'Whilst on a walked up shoot, I was very surprised by the large number of birds. I was smoking a Ramon Allones Specially Selected 4⅞th 50 ring gauge at the time. Having fired both barrels and needing to re-load quickly, I became confused and loaded my cigar into the right barrel instead of a new cartridge. Fortunately I was able to extract the cigar, but I failed to shoot the second wave of birds: a bit of a waste on two counts!'

David Lewis doesn't actually think that a particular cigar type matters. 'There is no "right" cigar for a shoot. It is all a matter of personal taste and what one is used to smoking. At the moment, large ring gauge cigars are very popular.' There is though, a 'right' way to prepare and smoke a cigar as David suggests: 'It is important to cut off the end of most cigars, i.e. those whose ends are not already cut, otherwise they will be impossible to smoke. Taking off the band has to be done very carefully otherwise the wrapper leaf can be torn, thereby ruining the draw – and the cigar. The cigar will shrink in girth whilst being smoked, so most smokers leave the band on until the cigar has been smoked about half-way.'

David also suggests some possible answers regarding 'cigar management':

'Cigar management during a drive, whether walked up or in a butt, is always a problem. There are several solutions, including the following:

◆ Always take a shooting stick and place the cigar in its saddle when the drive starts.

◆ If in a butt, place your cigar on the front of the butt, or alternatively give it, depending on the birds, to your loader.

◆ If all else fails: smoke and shoot, though health and safety tend to get exercised about this!'

### Buying cigars at auction

I have always been intrigued to know whether good quality cigars have ever been sold at auction in the same way as the wine cellars of the eminent and recently deceased. It seems they have, as Simon Chase told me that Havana cigars have customarily been auctioned along with wine cellars for many years, often by Christie's. Apparently, the record price for a Cuban cigar sold at auction was achieved in 2000, when some Partagas Lusitanias were sold for £1,000 each by Christie's. Although they are no longer involved, Cuban cigar auctions are still held regularly by some London cigar merchants.

Of course, wine, coffee, cigars, or indeed any other stimulants should be enjoyed with care, but nevertheless, I was much taken by the writing of W. Bromley-Davenport who, in 1888, observed the following regarding a certain type of young Gun in the shooting field: 'Dangerous as these excitable youths were, I have seen others more dangerous. Their excitability was natural, the result of too active and mercurial a temperament, and the danger arising out of it, though grave enough, was not quite so formidable as that caused by the artificially produced excitement of habitual over-indulgence in stimulants. One young man who had contracted this fatal habit, and was consequently haunted on occasions by visions of black beetles and crawling reptiles, was once heard to say, as he pushed back his chair after a breakfast consisting of a peach, a bottle of champagne and a glass of brandy, "There, I haven't eaten a heartier breakfast than that for a long time," had been shooting at a neighbour's of a host of mine. This young man... happened to be about thirty yards from a hollow lane along which a beater was proceeding carrying three or four hares on his back. They wobbled about as he walked, and the jumpy youth, catching sight of their movements, instantly fired a snap shot, with the effect of putting several pellets into the unhappy beater's back.'

◆

# Time for Tea

The chance for tea and cake after the last drive, even though it might follow fairly soon after a very substantial lunch, is much looked forward to by most Guns. It gives them a chance to talk about the day's sport and, should they be lucky enough to have been shooting with double guns, their loader the opportunity to clean the weaponry. Whatever the situation, this tradition allows for the last of the shot birds to be collected and the person in charge to arrive at a final score for the day.

It seems that Edwardian men were just as subject to ridicule by their fellow Guns as they are today during the end-of-day tea and cake session – but isn't good-natured banter and badinage the essence of any form of shooting or field sports? For those who indulged in the really big bag days of the early 1900s, a headache was a very real threat at tea-time – and not

**OPPOSITE TOP** A SOMEWHAT GRAND SLOVENIAN SHOOTING LODGE, WHERE GAME IS LAID OUT ON THE GRASSED AREA IN ORDER TO BE CEREMONIALLY COUNTED AND CELEBRATED
**BELOW LEFT** THERE IS A GROWING TREND TOWARDS ESTATES OFFERING GUEST GUNS PREVIOUSLY PREPARED BIRDS AS OPPOSED TO THOSE TAKEN DIRECTLY FROM THE GAME CART
**BELOW RIGHT** NO MATTER HOW GOOD THE LUNCH, THERE'S ALWAYS ROOM FOR A SLICE OF CAKE AND A CUP OF TEA AT THE END OF THE DAY

Abroad, Continental hunters will generally return to one of the many shooting lodges set in the woodland in order to count the game and take part in the traditional ceremonies associated with the end of the day (see *Counting the Bag – European-style* on page 158). The internal walls of such lodges are often decorated with trophies and general hunting paraphernalia, under which the hunters will gather to toast the success of the day – not for them a genteel cup of tea though; it is usually an occasion to imbibe some local fruit-based spirit which, incidentally, when drunk as a toast to the day, should always be held in the left hand, for some reason I have yet to fathom!

◆

because of what they'd been offered at lunch (in fact, the Edwardian Gun appears to have been a relatively abstemious creature) but more because of the number of shots he'd fired. Add to this the fact that he might well have been up until the early hours the night before playing cards and goodness knows what else, then a cup of tea could well have been the perfect antidote.

Incidentally, hunting in its many guises also has a tradition of taking tea after a day's sport and this practice is especially popular among beaglers who do not have a horse waiting outside to prick their consciences. The teas range from a spread of bread, cheese, pâtés, pies and cold meats through to cakes and crumpets, but above all the food will invariably be as calorific as it is reviving. The tea may be set out anywhere, from a private house to a pub or a village hall; or simply spread out over the bonnet of a hunt member's vehicle.

## TYPES OF TEA

The UK Tea Council claims on its website that, in 2737 BC, according to legend, a servant of the Emperor Shen Nung was boiling water in a cauldron when leaves from a nearby tea bush blew into his brew. On tasting the resulting drink Shen Nung found it delicious and continued to brew tea, drinking it as a medicinal tonic. An alternative history suggests that early Buddhist settlers in China chewed tea leaves as a prayer stimulant, but whatever the truth, tea had become a popular drink in China by the time of Confucius (551–479 BC). It began its worldwide spread in 900 AD, when the Japanese took up the habit of serving tea in intricate tea ceremonies, but it wasn't until the 1660s that the East India Company began to import tea into Britain. At first it was so expensive that a pound of tea cost the same as nine months' worth of labouring wages – no wonder it was kept under lock and key by those who *could* afford it!

Regarding the type of tea suitable for the end of a shooting day, Robert Armes (of the Rosie & Java Tea Company) suggests that it is well worth trying Ceylon Orange Pekoe, 'a traditional, clean-tasting, large-leaf black tea from Sri Lanka… also excellent is a good grade Darjeeling'. Robert adds, 'Earl Grey tea, with its immediately recognisable scent of bergamot, works very well with fish', therefore it would be good if smoked salmon sandwiches happen to be on the tea menu. 'But', says Robert: 'Above all, always drink good quality, good grade, loose-leaf teas. Life is too short to drink inferior quality dusty tea!'

Lapsang is possibly China's most famous tea and has a certain smoky aroma that supposedly comes from the ancient tradition of drying the leaves over pinewood fires; in reality, however, the smoked flavour comes from a process of rolling, oxidising and drying the leaves. Originally, oxidising green tea was done in order to ensure that it arrived in prime condition when exported to America and Europe.

In a book about shooting, it would be very remiss if Gunpowder tea wasn't included. This is another green tea which has been pan-fired and rolled into small pellets before drying. Looking very much like lead shot, the size of these pellets can vary considerably, from as small as a pinhead to as large as a garden pea. Black tea varieties include Yunnan, which has an earthy, malty taste and is best drunk with milk, and Keemun, which has a nutty aroma.

## *Brewing the perfect pot*

Taylors of Harrogate is an old established family business which was founded in 1886 by Charles Taylor. Nowadays, in addition to being one of the country's leading tea and coffee merchants, Taylors is also known for its restaurants – including the world-famous Bettys Café Tea Rooms. Who better then to offer advice on making the perfect pot of tea?

For all types of tea, use freshly-drawn water whenever possible – this ensures that the water has plenty of oxygen in it. As the water in the kettle is heated, pour a little into your teapot to warm it. Swirl, discard and follow the instructions below for Black Tea and Green Tea.

'END OF THE DAY' – A
WONDERFULLY EVOCATIVE
AND ATMOSPHERIC IMAGE BY
PROFESSIONAL PHOTOGRAPHER
COLIN BARKER
(© COLIN BARKER)

HOW THE GUNS HAND OVER A
TIP IS CRITICAL IN THE VIEW
OF MANY KEEPERS... MOST
PASS IT OVER DISCREETLY IN A
HANDSHAKE WHILST ACCEPTING
A BRACE OF BIRDS
(AGRIPIX LTD)

# A Place Fit for Purpose

Over the years I've been involved with shooting, I think I must have eaten everything from a squashed packet of sandwiches to *cordon bleu* cooking in every situation ranging from the leeward side of a dry-stone wall to the dining-room of a Scottish castle where we were served by a butler and immaculately dressed waiters. Just in case any party of Guns is currently contemplating the building or conversion of a lunch hut, no matter how large or small, here are a few random thoughts based on many years of experience. (Let us hope, though, that the reason for constructing a new shooting lodge is not as drastic as the one some years ago at the Llechweddygarth shoot, near Welshpool, Powys, which is owned by George and Carol Stott. Apparently while out shooting one day, George noticed that a fire had broken out in an estate barn. As a subsequent article in *The Field* phrased it: 'From this reversal

**OPPOSITE TOP** Pre-prandial drinks provide a perfect opportunity for some serious conversation (Courtesy of Christopher Hill)
**BELOW LEFT** Some mementoes of a bygone era
**BELOW RIGHT** A few cartridges left for the afternoon...

THE PURPOSE-BUILT FISHING AND SHOOTING LODGE AT DAMERHAM FISHERIES,
SET ON THE HAMPSHIRE/DORSET BORDER

of fortune Carol has created a charming shooting lodge. Guns are greeted by a wood-burning stove, excellent facilities and a welcome drink from George in the long, wood-panelled room.')

James Kelly, who is responsible for the shooting at Glenbuchat in Scotland, makes a very valid point when it comes to developing and kitting out a lodge with shooting clients in mind: 'Whilst Guns generally might be happy to accept a lodge with little or no home comforts if they are friends or family members, guests who are paying highly for their sport expect a little more.' In France, the ancient sporting estate of Parc de Launay was, for many years, quite neglected, until it was bought by Englishman Shaun Trenchard. He has converted the old shooting lodge into both a comfortable house for him and a wonderfully hospitable place for visiting Guns, with a warm and welcoming shoot room. The next door gun room is a treasure trove of interest too – containing a collection of rifle bullets and shotgun cartridges, photos of encounters with boar at, as far as I am concerned, distances far too close for comfort!

## THE SHOOT HUT

◆ To cut costs, it might be possible to construct a new shooting hut yourself, but otherwise the services of an architect should be employed. For most people, however, an off-the-peg model will be the favoured option – either supplied in sections to be built by a syndicate working party, or delivered and erected by the suppliers onto a suitable base that has been previously laid.

◆ Location is obviously important: the hut should be on flat ground, but not at the bottom of a slope for fear of flooding – although staddle-stones or a raised base could overcome this.

◆ Where possible, it should be south-facing and not directly under trees; it should, however, perhaps be discreetly situated so as to avoid unwanted attention – if necessary, consider fitting vandal-proof shutters over the windows and a roller-type metal locking door over the entrance.

◆ As to its overall size, whilst it obviously needs to provide a comfortable venue for the amount of people that will be using it, don't forget to bear in mind the fact that the outside dimensions will have to include the roof over-hang and the probable provision of water-butts and/or drainage to take away rainwater.

◆ Make sure that an adequate walkway from the car park to the entrance door is included: no one wants to arrive for that first cup of coffee or lunch-time drink having first had to negotiate mud and wet grass.

◆ If the hut is to serve as the meeting place at the beginning of the day, make sure that there is ample parking and that the early arrivals have the facilities for making themselves a cup of tea or coffee.

◆ Remember all the essentials and practicalities when contemplating a shoot hut: the type of flooring will dictate whether Wellingtons can be kept on (and if so, how is the floor to be kept regularly cleaned?), or whether it will be necessary for Guns to change into shoes before entering. Electricity or calor gas is a must for cooking – as is water; is there a practical way of supplying these?

◆ When run commercially, it may be necessary to include kitchen facilities that are of catering health and safety standards – and they may need to be inspected by local environment authorities.

◆ Incorporate a covered area where wet coats can be hung and boots removed for lunch, or before the drive home.

◆ Provided that it is in full view at all times, a traditional gun rack is a useful asset, as it saves shotguns from being left in cars and being trampled on by dogs. You might like to consider the provision of gun-cleaning equipment or, at the very least, a few soft cloths and a spray can or two of oil so that wet guns can be wiped off at midday.

◆ A log-burning stove is always appreciated. Try to organise for someone to tend to it

FROM THE SUBLIME TO THE RIDICULOUS – AT THE OPPOSITE END OF THE SCALE
TO DAMERHAM LODGE (PAGE 164). THIS RAMSHACKLE SHED IS USED AS A SHELTER
AND A PLACE FOR LUNCH BY COMMUNE GUNS IN FRANCE

halfway through the morning – there is nothing more dismal than returning to a fire that was burning well at the start of the day, only to find mere embers at lunchtime.

◆ A large dining table is essential: even if everyone sitting around it is eating their own sandwiches, a feeling of camaraderie is important and this will never be achieved if everyone has to split into groups in corners.

◆ Display in a prominent position an old-fashioned station or school-room clock: it is all too easy to forget the time and be late out for the first drive after lunch. This might not matter so much for the DIY shoot, but when beaters have gone out earlier than the Guns in order to do a little blanking-in, they do not want to be left cold and miserable waiting for the arrival of the Guns on the pegs.

◆ As a final touch, consider whether it is possible to include some form of kennelling. There is no reason why dogs shouldn't be as comfortable as you are during the lunch break and the provision of kennels will go a long way towards preventing smelly and steamed-up vehicles. Make sure that any bedding is clean – I have refused the offer of kennels on many occasions when I've seen straw litter that is obviously two or three seasons old and therefore the perfect breeding ground for fleas and mites.

## Construction Costs in the 1890s

When it comes to the cost and design of your lunch hut, I doubt that the invoice will compare very favourably with that of two huts built by Sir Allan Mackenzie in the late 1890s and which were described by Horace Hutchinson in 1903:

'Speaking of the Glenmuick moor recalls a memory of far the best form of luncheon hut or shelter that I ever have seen… It is made on the side of a hill remote from the prevailing wind. There is hardly a back wall to speak of, the slope of the hill, with a few feet cut away to get it perpendicular, giving this. Side walls, front wall, and roof all are made of fids of heathery turf bound together with strong twisted galvanised wire running on a strong rough woodwork. There are two thicknesses of turf throughout, and between the two is a sheet of paper felt, making the whole thing quite waterproof. The inner thickness of the turf has its heathery side towards the inside of the hut, and the outer thickness has its heathery side outwards, so that the whole thing within and without appears like the moorland itself grown into an artificial and extremely convenient shape. The whole is bound over on the outside with large-meshed wire netting to prevent the sheep and deer from pulling it to pieces.

'The most surprising point of it all is the cost. At a convenient distance from this luncheon hut Sir Allan Mackenzie has a less elaborate one of similar build for the loaders to have luncheon in, and the cost of the whole, calculating materials, men's time in building, etc., was only a five-pound note for the two. It is quite wonderful. The loaders' hut has a wooden bench running all round its semicircle, and it has no front wall or door. The shooters' magnificent hut has benches likewise and also a table running along its length. At each end, instead of continuing the benches, the seats have been made in the form of chests or boxes for stowing anything that is wanted. This simple but sufficient furniture is not included in the five-pound note which has done so much, but the cost of it can be but a few pounds additional.'

# How to Get It Wrong!

Written with tongue firmly in cheek, this concluding chapter of *The Shoot Lunch* provides an object lesson in how not to behave. Every single one of the examples given is based on true first-hand experiences, gathered over almost forty years of involvement with game shooting in its many forms. Following the behaviour described below will most certainly ensure that you are never asked shooting to the same place twice: conversely, do the exact opposite, and you'll be sure of a succession of invitations!

**1** When you first receive your invitation, do not worry too much about responding straight away – a day on a (prestigious or otherwise) shoot is no big deal. Just text a reply to your would-be host if and when you think of it or, if you feel it really necessary, perhaps wait and give him a phone call a couple of days before the date. If he's any sort of host, he'll fit you in as an extra Gun in the line, as he'd assumed you weren't coming and has therefore invited someone else in your place. This won't cause too many problems on the day.

**2** Develop a habit of being late at any meeting place; your host and fellow sportsmen will learn to love your individualism and you will soon become recognised as being a bit of a maverick with a mind of your own.

On arrival at the shoot, it is probably best if you let your dog out straight away. If you've had a long journey, it will appreciate the chance to cock its leg on the boots of a fellow Gun and to empty its bowels on your host's lawn. Better still, it gives the dog a chance to stretch its legs before the day starts, especially if it can run into a bit of nearby cover and loosen up a little by chasing a few birds about.

**3** Get to know any new Guns by going around each one and telling them your life story. It is far more important to do this than it is to go and say 'good morning' to your host or shoot captain. Your fellow Guns will love to know more about you and will probably be absolutely fascinated by your accounts of recent shooting days when you shot the highest pheasant, or bowled over a bolting rabbit that ran through the gun line. Please don't worry about rushing to get yourself into your shooting coat and outdoor boots because the rest of the team will be more than happy to wait until you are ready to move off.

It might perhaps be useful to listen to the pre-shoot talk but should you miss this particular one, it's probably of no consequence – they are, after all, similar to the flight crew's safety instructions on an aeroplane and, once you've heard one, you've heard them all.

**4** At the first drive, slam your vehicle door and, if at all possible, delay getting to your gun peg by carrying on with any conversations that you may have previously started. Where possible, do so in a loud voice as this, combined with the door slamming, will help in making the pheasants wary and possibly turning them away from the direction in which they are being driven. This conservation of game will be much appreciated by the beaters who will gain the benefit when it comes to their days at the end of the season. Once the birds start coming, shoot only the low ones and, if you can, try and kill all those that are flying directly over your neighbours.

**5** One of the great joys of shooting is the camaraderie it engenders. Therefore, if, after the end of a particularly good first drive, you find yourself short of cartridges, since you didn't expect your host to be able to show you more than half a dozen birds throughout the day, just borrow some more from your fellow guests. They won't mind at all if it leaves their cartridge bags empty later on in the day, as you can rest assured that they will feel a warm glow of satisfaction in watching you killing pheasants with their ammunition.

**6** Your dog should, if you've done as suggested at the beginning of the day, be nicely excited by now, particularly if you let it pick up any shot game as the drive is in progress. It is really good to have a pile of birds at the base of your peg before the drive is finished and your neighbouring Guns (especially those with dogs of their own) will be very grateful for the fact that they have no birds to collect.

If you prefer, it is permissible to tie your dog to your cartridge bag or to the gun peg as it will give your new friends great amusement to watch the dog disappear through the nearest hedge scattering spilt cartridges or trailing a place marker. A dog that squeaks and whines at the peg is much appreciated by your host as he will be in no doubt that at least one of his guests is having a good time. Remember, too, that it is important to utilise any and every opportunity to shout loudly and often at your dog.

**7** Between drives, you might like to criticise the way things are going. This is always appreciated by fellow Guns and your host but, most of all, by the keeper or person in charge of organising the beaters and planning the overall running of the day, who will be delighted to listen to your suggestions and ideas. If you are really lucky, he might be able to give you some suggestions of his own.

**8** If you are on a shoot where numbers have been drawn and everyone moves up two or three numbers for each drive, it can be great fun to forget your next number and confuse everyone by insisting that you should be standing on a particular peg – even if the person already standing there is convinced that he is in the correct place. If all else fails, the host or shoot captain will be on hand and he or she will, of course, be able to remember the number with which each and every Gun started the day.

**9** A shooting lunch might be a bundle of pre-packed sandwiches eaten in a farmyard barn, or a fine sit-down affair in your host's dining-room. If the latter, do not bother to remove your muddy boots in favour of clean shoes kept in the car for just such occasions and please, don't worry about allowing your muddy dog access to the table – after all, the rest of the Guns will be animal lovers and therefore not likely to mind their lunch being disturbed by a begging, slobbering dog. It is far better to get muddy paw marks on your host's carpet than it is to risk dirtying the interior of your car by putting your dog in there during the lunch break. If your host offers wine, remember to drink plenty of it during lunch – he might be offended if you do not and anyway, drinking heavily at lunchtime is bound to improve your aim in the afternoon. The majority of Guns these days are non-smoking: should you not be, don't worry, a coffee cup makes the perfect ashtray.

**10** Finally, in order to be really certain that you'll never be invited back, don't bother to thank the beaters and pickers-up at the end of the day – they get paid to do their job anyway. Whilst on the subject of money; although it is traditional to tip the keeper or person in charge of the beating line when thanking him for a wonderful day's sport, it is not really necessary – especially if you don't need to see him in order to collect the customary brace of game.

If you do decide to tip the keeper, make a big thing of handing over the money in full view of everybody. You might notice some of your fellow Guns handing over £10 or £20 notes but do not allow yourself to be swayed by such largesse – a few coins will go a long way towards ensuring that your visit will be remembered for a very long time to come...

## MANNERS MAKETH MAN

Sadly, modern commercialism has, at least in part, been responsible for some less than gentlemanly behaviour out shooting. Jonathan Young, editor-in-chief of *The Field*, describes in one article an instance where a certain Gun cut off every single bird climbing towards his neighbour. None of the pheasants he shot were challenging and all would have made a better shot had they not been reduced to feathered clumps on the plough. Some people appear to think 'Well, I have paid for my share and I'm going to shoot it'.

It is surely far better to regard every day out with the gun as a treat to be treasured and to follow the example of our Victorian and Edwardian predecessors who were apparently given to excessive bouts of politeness and consideration. At this time there was, according to Anthony Vandervell and Charles Coles, writing in *Game and the English Landscape*, a new etiquette that supposedly separated the true gentleman from the rest. In fact, as they remark in the text, '...some delightful prose and loose verse was written to illustrate the finer points of order. "Better a bird spared than a bird shared" became the rule; and afterwards, when picking up game, "Gentlemen, whilst upon the moors, don't say 'That's mine' – but 'Here's yours' "'.

◆

**OPPOSITE**
TRY NEVER TO RUN SHORT OF CARTRIDGES

# Bibliography and Sources

Ayrton, Elisabeth (and others): *Farmhouse Cookery, Recipes from the Country Kitchen.* Readers Digest Association Ltd, 1980

Beeton, Isabella: *Mrs Beeton's Book of Household Management.* 1861

Bertam, J. G: *Outdoor Sports in Scotland.* 1889

Billett, Michael: *A History of English Country Sports.* Robert Hale, 1994

Bromley-Davenport, W.: *Sport* (new edition). Chapman and Hall Ltd, 1888

Colegate, Isabel: *The Shooting Party.* Hamish Hamilton, 1980/Penguin Modern Classics, 2007

Davidson, Alan: *Oxford Companion to Food.* Oxford University Press, 1999

Fisher, M. J.: *Liqueurs: A Dictionary and Survey.* Maurice Meyer Ltd, 1951

Fourin, Pierre: *Glen Tanar: Valley of Echoes and Hidden Treasures.* Leopard Magazine Publishing 2009

Hardy, Valentine and de Randolph, Philippe: *The Lost Poems of W. H. Kennings.* Blackwell Press, 2005

Hargreaves, Barbara (editor): *The Country Book.* Countrywise Books, Agricultural Press Ltd, 1971

Harris, John: *No Voice from the Hall: Early Memories of a Country House Snooper.* John Murray, 1988

Hartley, Mary and Ingilby, Joan: *A Dales Heritage.* Dalesman Books, 1982

Hasted, E.: *The History and Topographical Survey of Kent.* 1782

Hobson, J. C. Jeremy and Watts, Philip: *Cook Game.* Crowood Press, 2008

Hobson, J. C. Jeremy and Watts, Philip: *The New Country Cook.* Crowood Press, 2009

Holt, Peter: *The Keen Shot's Miscellany.* Quiller, 2008

Humphreys, John: *The Complete Game Shoot.* David & Charles, 1992

Hutchins, Sheila: *Pâtés & Terrines.* Elm Tree Books, 1978

Hutchinson, Horace G. (editor and contributor): *Shooting.* The Country Life Library of Sport, 1903

Jefferies, Richard: *The Gamekeeper at Home.* 1878 (and countless reprints since)

Jones, Owen: *Ten Years of Game-Keeping.* Edward Arnold 1909

Keith, E. C.: *Gun For Company.* Country Life Ltd, 1937

*Larousse Gastronomique.* Updated and revised edition, Hamlyn 2009

Loch Fyne Whiskies: summer 2010 brochure.

Mahon, Katie: 'Mr Bunbury's shooting lunches' – an article in *Country Illustrated,* November 1997

Marriat-Ferguson, J. E.: *Visiting Home.* Published privately, 1905

Martin, Brian: *Tales of the Old Gamekeepers.* David & Charles, 1989

Martin, Brian: *The Great Shoots; Britain's Premier Sporting Estates.* David & Charles, 1987 Revised 2nd edition Quiller, 2007

Mayhew, Henry: *London Labour and the London Poor.* 1851 (available as a Penguin Classic, 1985)

Miller, Christian: *A Childhood in Scotland.* John Murray, 1981

Musson, Jeremy: *Up and Down Stairs: The History of the Country House Servant.* John Murray 2009

Nickerson, Rosie: *How to be Asked Again.* Quiller, 2009

O' Connor, Kaori: *The English Breakfast.* Revised 2nd edition, Kegan Paul, 2006

Otho Paget, J. (and others): *Horses, Guns and Dogs.* George Allen, 1903

Paterson, Jennifer and Dickson Wright, Clarissa: *Two Fat Ladies – Gastronomic Adventures (with motorbike and sidecar).* Ebury Press, 1996

Pirie, Charlie, with Iain Fraser Grigor: *The Gamekeeper – A Year in the Glen.* BBC Books, 1995

Radclyffe, C. R. E.: *Shooting.* (Personal memoirs printed and published dates unknown)

Roberts, Alasdair: *Midges.* Birlinn Ltd, 1998 (reprinted and revised 2005)

Ruffer, Jonathan Garnier: *The Big Shots; Edwardian Shooting Parties.* Quiller, 1977

Smullen, Ivor: *Taken for a Ride – A Distressing Account of the Misfortunes and Misbehaviour of the Early British Railway Traveller.* Herbert Jenkins, 1968

Spottiswoode, J.: *The Moorland Gamekeeper.* David & Charles, 1977

Stanford, J. K.: *The Wandering Gun.* Geoffrey Bles Ltd 1960

*The Field*: various articles. IPC Magazines.

Vandervell, Anthony and Coles, Charles: *Game and the English Landscape; The Influence of the Chase on Sporting Art and Scenery.* Debrett's Peerage Ltd, 1980

Weld, Charles: *Two Months in the Highlands.* 1860